ONE
FOR THE
AGES

THE 2001 BASEBALL SEASON IN WORDS AND PICTURES

ONE FOR THE AGES

DAVE ROSENBAUM

ALBION PRESS

ALBION PRESS • TAMPA, FLORIDA

ONE FOR THE AGES

Copyright © 2002 by Dave Rosenbaum

All rights reserved. No part of this book may be reproduced without prior written permission from the publisher, except for brief excerpts to be used for review purposes.

ALBION PRESS
4532 West Kennedy Blvd., Suite 233
Tampa, FL 33609

ISBN 0-9709-170-4-X

Library of Congress Cataloging-in-Publication Data

Rosenbaum, Dave, 1960–
   One for the ages : the 2001 baseball season in words and pictures / Dave Rosenbaum.
      p. cm.
   ISBN 0-9709170-4-X
   1. Baseball—United States. 2. Baseball players—United States.
I. Title.
   GV863.A1 R587 2002
   796.357'0973—dc21
   2002001290

Cover photos (used with permission):
   • Randy Johnson: Brian Bahr, Allsport
   • Cal Ripken and Barry Bonds: Otto Gruele, Allsport
Cover design by Bob Antler, Antler Designworks
Book design and composition by John Reinhardt Book Design

Printed in Canada

CONTENTS

Introduction vii

THE PLAYERS
1. Ichiro Suzuki 1
2. Albert Pujols 15
3. Roger Clemens 23
4. Sammy Sosa 33
5. Randy Johnson 41
6. Alex Rodriguez 49
7. Rickey Henderson 57
8. Tony Gwynn 65
9. Cal Ripken Jr. 73
10. Barry Bonds 83

THE TEAMS
11. Seattle Mariners 101
12. New York Mets 115
13. New York Yankees 125

THE WORLD SERIES
14. The Greatest World Series Ever 137

Bonds Catches McGwire 159
Broken records 163

INTRODUCTION

THIS SPORT SURE CAN TAKE A PUNCH. It wasn't meant for the toughest people in the world, but baseball refuses to go quietly. It wasn't meant for the fastest people in the world, but here it is, up and sprinting in the early part of the 21st century. It wasn't meant for the strongest people in the world, but has any sport in the history of North America ever packed more muscle? No way. The people who care for it keep trying to kill it, and baseball comes up with the trick answer every time. Idiot-proof, is what it is.

The game was done, finished, through, the naysayers said, after a labor dispute in 1994 caused the cancellation of the World Series—an event as anticipated by many Americans as Thanksgiving, Christmas and the Fourth of July. Fans by the millions turned away from the National Pastime. And surely it was dead for good after the 1997 season, when Florida Marlins owner Wayne Huizenga bought the players he needed to win the World Series, then got rid of them after Game Seven was won. A sport could never survive such chutzpah, such crass behavior, such lack of respect by its owners.

The Major Leagues kept adding more teams, resulting in a watering down of talent, especially pitching. So what happened? The sport turned a positive into a negative. Very good hitters turned into sensational sluggers, feeding off sub-par pitching, and offense soared. In 1998, Mark McGwire and Sammy Sosa spent the season trying to reach Roger Maris's record of 61 homeruns in a season, and fans couldn't help but watch. The game wasn't hurt by the fact that McGwire was as strong as Superman, and Sosa was as likable as a favorite cousin. McGwire not only smashed the record, he hit a magical number, a number nobody thought would ever be reached—70—and the game was back on solid ground.

Or so it seemed. After a thrilling 2000 season highlighted by a Subway Series between the New York Yankees and New York Mets, the owners and players continued to heap abuse on baseball, as the Texas Rangers signed free-agent shortstop Alex Rodriguez for $252-million over ten years. Such greed. Such disregard for what used to be the right way to build a winner: through trades and a team's minor league system.

And, even during what turned out to be an unforgettable 2001 season, the owners and players couldn't help themselves. There was talk of a players strike or owners lockout before or during the 2002 season. Commissioner Bud Selig kept bringing up the subject of contraction—meaning some teams had to go—while the rest of us were trying to enjoy a season that defied description. Couldn't those silly owners and players simply shutup and play?

But we shouldn't have been surprised by baseball's resiliency. After all, this is the sport that survived the Black Sox scandal in 1919, when the Chicago White Sox allegedly threw the World Series.

What happened in 2001? Well, take a deep breath, and try to appreciate the fact that all of these things happened not in one century, or one decade, but in one season.

A player broke the record for most homeruns in a season.

A rookie from Japan set the Major League record for hits in a season.

A rookie from the Dominican Republic broke the rookie record for most RBIs in a season.

One of the most disliked veterans in baseball broke Ty Cobb's career record for runs scored and Babe Ruth's career record for walks.

Another pitcher set the American League career strikeouts record.

A $252-million man set the record for most homeruns in a season by a shortstop.

Two of the most beloved players in recent history retired.

A team that lost its three best players over the past three seasons tied the Major League record for wins in a season and smashed the American League record.

A fourth-year team won the most exciting World Series ever played.

More? Certainly. Two of sports history's most lovable losers, the Boston Red Sox and the Chicago Cubs, convinced their fans that this might be *the* year that hearts stopped breaking. The Sox, just a half game out in the American League East at the All-Star break, proceded to fire their manager, lose 13 out of 14 games in late August and early September and finish thirteen and a half games behind the Yankees while missing the playoffs. In typical Red Sox fashion, they won their last five games when nothing mattered.

As for the Cubs, with Sosa leading the way, they pulled an even bigger tease by taking the National League Central lead into September, then missing the playoffs entirely.

Two records that remained intact in 2001: the Cubs haven't won the World Series since 1907, the Red Sox since 1918.

Truly, the 2001 season was one in which we watched ESPN every night to find out the score and eagerly waited for our morning newspapers to read all about it. We kept saying that we had outgrown the game, and yet its pull proved irresistable throughout. We found players to watch, even though we kept telling ourselves that these guys were multi-millionaires who didn't give a damn about the rest of us. We ignored reality and got lost in the fantasy.

Wrote Jim Caple of ESPN.com, "Baseball's toughest trivia question is whether 2001 was one of the game's greatest years or one of its worst. What do you say about a year in which we sat under a warming sun in McCovey Cove, waiting for history to land in our rowboats, and also squirmed in our seats under oath at a Congressional hearing, waiting for Selig to answer a question honestly? What do you say about a year in which the stadium where Bonds tied McGwire's record is named for a bankrupt company [Enron Field] that apparently cooked its books? What do you say about a year in which we plucked home run baseballs from the air and held them to our hearts only to have the commissioner order fans in Minnesota and Montreal to throw them back? The year's schizophrenia was best exemplified by the Bonds chase. Should we have embraced Bonds for his great career? Or given him the cold shoulder he so often turned toward the fans?"

Of course, the question of whether 2001 was baseball's greatest year or its worst was settled on September 11, the date of the worst terrorist attack in United States history. Two planes crashed into the World Trade Center, one crashed into the Pentagon, and one crashed into a field in western Pennsylvania, resulting in the deaths of over 3,000 people. The season was interrupted for only the third time in history, aside from labor disputes and weather. (The other two times were August 2, 1923, when President Warren G. Harding died, and June 6, 1944, when Allied forces invaded France in World War II. The 1989 World Series was postponed ten days after San Francisco's earthquake.)

"That was terrible," Selig said. "This transcends it in a horrific way beyond human comprehension."

When the games resumed on September 17, each team observed moments of silence before its remaining games, teams gave their fans American flags and sang "God Bless America" instead of "Take Me Out To The Ballgame" during the seventh-inning stretch and every player wore an American flag on his uniform. The players, seemingly embarrassed by what they do for a living after such a tragic event, openly displayed their emotions, and teams millions of fans in the heartland of America never would have dreamed of rooting for—the Yankees and the Mets—became emblematic of American patriotism because the two teams represented New York, Ground Zero of the tragedy.

So the 2001 Major League Baseball season wasn't the greatest ever. The word "great" can't be used to describe a year in which so many people died tragically. And by no means was it the worst. Not with so many thrilling events happening on the field almost daily. Quantifying this season is impossible.

It was simply one for the ages.

THE PLAYERS

1

ICHIRO SUZUKI
THE JAPANESE CYCLONE
WHO BLEW THROUGH THE MAJORS

In the on-deck circle, he swings his bat in arcs, rotating it around and around, almost as if he intends on using it as a Samurai sword. The focus of attention in the game is on the pitcher on the mound and the batter at the plate, but in the stadium, most of the fans, and all of a contingent of seventy writers and photographers from Japan, have turned their eyes to the on-deck circle, more interested in the next hitter than the current one. Ichiro Suzuki has entered the spotlight he never wanted in the first place.

Next, he stretches, placing his arms and Mizuno baseball bat behind his back. Stretching is one of the things he does best, because he does it so frequently. When his turn at-bat arrives, he walks slowly to the plate, stops, plants his feet outside his shoulders—a wide stance—and slowly lowers his upper body to the ground, and if he's sitting on an invisible stool. In Japanese martial arts, this is called the horse stance, and its purpose is to establish one's center of gravity. Ichiro is about to strike.

With his left foot in the batter's box, Ichiro waves his bat back and forth below his belt, as if he's playing golf and the next putt is

(Opposite page) Ichiro didn't bunt much in Japan because he was a power hitter, but in the American League, he showed that he could reach base every way possible.

for par. Then he whips it around counterclockwise and stops when his hands reach his chest. With his right hand, he holds the weapon parallel to his upper body, then he brings his right foot into the batter's box. His knees are bent. His left elbow, the front one, is cocked high. He's ready for the pitch. All eyes are focused on him.

He repeats this ceremony before every pitch, yet this picture of efficiency is all motion once the play starts. The pitcher delivers. Ichiro swings. Quite often, he makes contact, and he seems to be moving toward first base even before he completes his swing. It seems unfair. With everything else he does right, Ichiro has a running start.

"Some people may think it's strange," Ichiro said, "but if something works, there's no need to change."

No need to change a thing. In 2001, Ichiro Suzuki, the first Japanese-born position player in the Major Leagues, led the Majors with a .350 batting average, joining Tony Oliva of the Minnesota Twins as the only rookies to win a batting title. Ichiro's MLB-leading 56 stolen bases made him the first player in either league to lead both categories since Jackie Robinson in 1949. He also set the MLB rookie record with 242 hits and established AL rookie records with 192 singles and 692 at-bats, led in multi-hit games with 75 and finished among the league leaders in runs (second), total bases (ninth) and triples (tied for seventh).

He batted .445, a Major League-best, with runners in scoring position, and his 23-game hit streak tied for the longest in both leagues. Ichiro's 242 hits were a Seattle Mariners club record and the most in the Majors since 1930, when Bill Terry had 254 for the New York Giants.

He won the Gold Glove for his defensive skills in rightfield.

He was named American League Rookie of the Year, even though at age 27 with seven Japanese batting titles behind him, he was hardly a typical rookie.

He won the American League Most Valuable Player award, making him only the second player in MLB history to win Rookie of the Year and MVP in the same year. Fred Lynn (1975 with Boston) was the other.

But, perhaps most importantly, batting in the leadoff position, he helped the Mariners forget departed shortstop Alex Rodriguez and helped Seattle to a record 116-win season and a spot in the American League Championship Series.

"It's very simple," Mariners centerfielder Mike Cameron said. "Time and time again, Ichiro has been our go-to guy. He hits, we win."

The only thing typical about Ichiro was his last name, which in Japan is as common as Jones is in the United States. That's why only Ichiro—which means fast man—appears on the back of his jersey, and why he prefers to be called Ichiro and nothing but Ichiro. Nine Japanese players were on Major League rosters during the 2001 season, but only two—Ichiro and New York Mets outfielder Tsuyoshi Shinjo—were position players, and only Ichiro took the game by storm. A superstar in Japan, where he is revered by fans and had his childhood home turned into a museum, he left Japan for one simple reason—"It just wasn't interesting anymore"—and embraced the challenge of proving that Japanese position players could hit in American baseball.

"He's at such a level of baseball that he needed to be here," San Francisco Giants slugger Barry Bonds said. "If he didn't make the move he did, he could have gotten bored."

"He's a pioneer, like Lewis and Clark," Mariners manager Lou Piniella said.

Ichiro the Pioneer was followed even more closely in the United States, where reporters are allowed into the clubhouse before and after games, than he was in Japan, where reporters aren't allowed into the clubhouse and rely on milquetoast quotes fed to them by club officials. Nearly a hundred Japanese reporters followed Ichiro during spring training. The Mariners issued press credentials to 39 Japanese news outlets for the 2001 season. Forty Japanese reporters and photographers made the Mariners' first road trip to Texas and saw Ichiro get four hits and hit his first Major League home run against the Rangers. Japan's government-owned NHK network broadcast every Mariners game to homes in Japan with high-definition receivers and about 55 home and away games to conventional TV. *Sports Illustrated* magazine told the story of Ichiro's first day of spring training, when a Japanese reporter told one of the Mariners' coaches, "Ichiro take 216 swings today." The next day, the reporter inquired about whether Ichiro was injured because he took only 187 swings.

"He's different from other baseball players," NHK producer Yuji Kato told *Newsday*. "He has spiky hair and sunglasses like a rock star in the States. He represents the full range of generations in Japan. He's like a son that we're sending off to an American college."

The difference is, of course, than when a son goes off to an American college, he comes back wearing the sweatshirts and caps of his university. In Seattle, baseball fans didn't mind shelling out $125 apiece for Mariners jerseys with Ichiro's number, 51, and first name on the back. Ichiro jerseys sold as well as A-Rod, Ken Griffey Jr. and Randy Johnson jerseys had in the past.

All this for a guy who's 5'9" and weighs 160 pounds soaking wet.

"I've never seen anybody like him," teammate Bret Boone said.

The Mariners paid dearly for their pioneer, making a $13.1-million payment in November 2000 to Ichiro's former team, the Orix BlueWave, for the right to negotiate with Ichiro and $14-million for a three year contract. He had played nine seasons in Japan, winning seven straight Pacific League batting titles, three league MVPs and seven Gold Gloves. In 2000, he hit a Pacific League record .387. The Mariners had seen him before in person. He got his first taste of the Majors in 1999, when they invited him to work out during spring training.

"I felt like a little kid," Ichiro said through his translator. "I wanted to play in the majors as soon as possible."

From his first game in spring training 2001, he was obviously a player different from any American baseball fans had ever seen. A special player? Nobody knew about that, but he had a different way of doing things.

He was quiet, refusing to speak to the media before games, and turning his back to reporters while answering questions at his clubhouse locker after games (a common rumor was that a Japanese

(Opposite page) Ichiro Suzuki, the leading vote-getter for the 72nd All-Star Game at Safeco Field in Seattle, is the center of media attention before the game. Suzuki proved he belonged by leading off the first inning with a single off National League starter Randy Johnson.

publication had offered a big reward for pictures of Ichiro naked). There was his habit of using a wooden carrot-shaped stick to pound his feet and keep them in shape ("If your feet are healthy, you're healthy," he said), his practice of cleaning his glove after every game, his intense stretching in the on-deck circle and his batting style.

"He's got a unique batting approach, where it looks like he's almost running out of the box as he hits the ball," Mariners first baseman John Olerud said as the season wore on and Ichiro failed to find a pitcher he couldn't hit. "I think the amazing thing is how he's been able to stay so consistent. A lot of these pitchers he hasn't seen before, but he's got such hand-eye coordination that he's able to put the bat on the ball, fight off tough pitches and keep the at-bat alive."

"He's a player," Piniella said. "He's a professional hitter."

And a professional fielder who had a routine in rightfield, too. Between every pitch, he'd roll his shoulders, stretch his quads and bend at the waist and touch his toes, always doing everything possible to be ready for whatever happened. There was seemingly no wasted time in his life. He never watched TV for a long time without wearing sunglasses. Better to protect his valuable eyes. Before every game, a Mariners trainer gave him a massage.

Well, he was worth pampering.

On Opening Day in Seattle, the Mariner and A's were tied 4-4 in the bottom of the eighth. With a man on first, Ichiro, who has surprising speed for a guy who was known for his power in Japan, reached on a bunt single to key the game-winning rally. It was the first time he had bunted in seven years.

"He's probably one of the greatest bunters in the world," Ted Heid, the Mariners' Director of Pacific Rim Operations, told *Sports Illustrated*. "But people didn't pay to watch him bunt. It would be like Mark McGwire bunting. They came to watch him hit."

Ichiro went hitless in four at-bats in the Mariners' second game, but had two hits in the third game to move over .300. He wouldn't be under .300 for the rest of the season. In the tenth inning of a game in Texas on April 6th, Ichiro got around on an inside pitch and hit the game-winning home run. He would hit safely in fifteen

straight games and go 4-for-4 against the Rangers on April 17, nearly overshadowing A-Rod's return to Seattle. His first home-run was a tenth-inning game winner in Texas. He had 30 hits in the Mariners' first 19 games and was named American League Rookie of the Month for April. Meanwhile, the Mariners were the hottest team in baseball. A Japanese tourist attraction, too.

"I'll be sitting in my office at Safeco where we have a big picture outside of Ichiro, and a tour bus will pull up," club president Chuck

Armstrong told *Newsday*. "You'll see everyone get out of the bus and take pictures of themselves in front of Ichiro's picture, then get back on the bus."

He fielded, he ran. The Mariners timed him getting from home to first in a very fast 3.7 seconds. He threw, making a 200-foot throw from rightfield to third on April 11 to nail Oakland's Terrence Long. Two nights later in Anaheim, he ended the Angels' eighth-inning rally when he climbed the wall to catch Tim Salmon's drive, then doubled Orlando Palmeiro off first base. He hit.

"He has the ability to get hits inside both lines and in both gaps," Mets manager Bobby Valentine said. Valentine had watched Ichiro play in Japan and had called him one of the five greatest players in the world. "And he'll get infield hits. He's also exciting, a player you'd pay to watch."

Ichiro never cooled off. In mid-May, he had back-to-back single-double-triple games which completed his 23-game hitting streak. When that streak ended, one game short of the franchise record, Ichiro declared, "This is not the end of my career," and started another streak, hitting in 12 of 13 games. He missed only two games prior to the All-Star break and, thanks to a flurry of votes from his home country, was the leading vote-recipient for the All-Star Game. Of course, by that time, the man whose quick bat, dazzling speed and flashy fielding earned him the nickname "The Wizard," deserved to be there. He was hitting .345.

"He's a legitimate hitter, no question," Yankees manager Joe Torre said. "I don't think you can pitch him one way. You can go in and out, up and down and he makes the adjustment. You can get ahead in the count, and Suzuki still seems relaxed. He doesn't seem to have any weaknesses."

"I've always been very confident," Ichiro said. "I'm just doing what I know how to do."

Ichiro never cooled off. From August 1st on, his average never dropped below .330 after a night's work. Against the Cleveland Indians in the American League Division Series, Ichiro batted a series record .600, scored four runs and drove in three more runs to help Seattle win in five games. In the decisive fifth game, he

ICHIRO SUZUKI CAREER STATISTICS

- Height: 5'11"
- Weight: 157 lbs.
- Throws: Right
- Bats: Left
- Born: October 22, 1973, Kasugai, Japan

SEASON	TEAM	G	AB	R	H	2B	3B	HR	RBI	BB	SO	SB	CS	OBP	SLG	OPS	AVG
2001	SEATTLE	157	692	127	242	34	8	8	69	30	53	56	14	.381	.457	.838	.350

singled in the seventh inning and scored to give the Mariners some breathing room in a 3-1 win. When Ichiro stopped hitting in the American League Championship Series against the Yankees, getting only four hits in 18 at-bats, the Mariners went down with him, losing in five games.

At that point, only two questions remained: Would Ichiro win the American League MVP? Would he win the American League Rookie of the Year, even though he was hardly a typical, inexperienced rookie? Yes to the first question. A resounding yes to the second, too: He received all but one of the 28 first-place votes for Rookie of the Year. Only Chris Assenheimer of the *Chronicle-Telegram* in Elyria, Ohio, submitted his first-place vote for 21-year-old Indians lefty C.C. Sabathia, insisting that Ichiro wasn't a rookie.

"I'm not surprised at all by the results, but to be honest with you, if I won this award, I had wanted to win it unanimously," Ichiro said. "Looking back at what I have done—I played nine years in Japan—I was a little embarrassed to be called a rookie here in the United States. This was the first time playing in the United States, except the time when I played in winter ball in Hawaii. Maybe I was a rookie this year."

For MVP, Ichiro beat out A's first baseman Jason Giambi in one of the closest races in Major League history.

"I didn't know how much my defense and running would influence the voters," Ichiro said, "I think my defense and running makes me a good player."

Now, Ichiro's name is being associated with Mickey Mantle, Ted Williams, Lou Gehrig and other all-time greats. He has become a pioneer who paved a golden road.

"To be among those great legends, great players, I cannot be an ordinary player anymore," Ichiro said.

He was never ordinary in the first place.

LAND OF THE RISING SONS

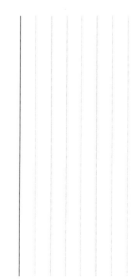

IF ICHIRO SUZUKI WAS THE PIONEER, the first Japanese-born position player in Major League Baseball history, then Tsuyoshi Shinjo of the New York Mets was right on his trail. Shinjo became the second Japanese position player to ink a contract with a Major League team when he signed with the Mets in December 2000. Shinjo wasn't nearly as successful as Ichiro in his first MLB season, but he excited fans with his flashy style and outstanding play in outfield.

The 29-year-old free-swinging righthander was a regular in New York's starting lineup and batted .268 with 10 homers and 56 RBIs. He left spring training in March as the Mets' fourth outfielder, but injuries to Benny Agbayani and Timo Perez gave him his chance. Shinjo took advantage and homered in the Mets' home-opener.

Shinjo and Ichiro Suzuki were the only non-pitchers among the nine Japanese players on Major League rosters, but they weren't the only ones who made an impact.

In early April, Anaheim Angels reliever Shigetoshi Hasegawa pitched to Ichiro, marking the first time a Japanese pitcher had thrown a Major League pitch to a Japanese batter. Ichiro reached on an infield single.

On April 4, Boston Red Sox righthander Hideo Nomo, the second player from Japan to play in the majors when he came up with the Los Angeles Dodgers in 1995, pitched his second no-hitter, a 3-0 victory over the Baltimore Orioles.

Mariners closer Kazuhiro Sasaki, the 2000 Rookie of the Year, was second in the American League with 45 saves.

"There are guys over there who can not only play in our league but can also be a big part of it, and you're going to see more and more," Angels manager Mike Scioscia said. "These guys are going to make their mark in the majors."

Why? How? Until the mid-1990s, the only Japanese player to ever appear on a Major League roster in America was pitcher Masanori

Murakami, who was 5-1 with the 1964 San Francisco Giants. Murakami returned home to Japan the following season, and Major League Baseball didn't host another Japanese player for thirty years.

"We are a little bit of a closed-door society," Hide Sueyoshi, Ichiro's translator, told *The Christian Science Monitor*. "Thirty, forty years ago, we did not have much information about Major-League-Baseball. But now you get live coverage of American games. Players realized that this is the highest level where they can compete. We see the power hitting here and a different kind of baseball, and we are fascinated by that."

In 1995, pitcher Hideo Nomo signed with the Los Angeles Dodgers, drew sellout crowds for his starts at Dodgers Stadium, and won 43 games in three seasons, proving a Japanese player could not only compete in America, but could star. Now, slowly but surely, other Japanese players are making the jump, and teams are eager to have them.

Kansas City Royals pitcher Mac Suzuki was the first player from Japan to begin his career in the American minor leagues, and he did it before Nomo ever landed on American shores. He played two seasons with independent teams in California before Seattle signed him as a free-agent following the 1993 season. Although this Suzuki hasn't made a major impact on the game like Ichiro has, he has appeared in 110 games since 1996.

"Before I came here, not any Japanese players were in the big leagues," Suzuki said. "I came here and three years later Nomo came. Before that, Japanese players never thought about it, that they can play. This is a dream, a Japanese player playing American baseball. And I came here, Nomo came, [Hideki] Irabu came, everybody came."

In addition to Ichiro Suzuki, these Japanese-born players played in the Major Leagues in 2001:

Tsuyoshi Shinjo, outfielder, New York Mets. He batted .268 in 123 games with 10 homers and 56 RBIs. Traded to the Giants during the off-season.

Kaz Sasaki, relief pitcher, Seattle Mariners. His 45 saves were second in the American League.

Hideo Nomo, starting pitcher, Boston Red Sox. Pitched the second no-hitter of his career in April. Finished with a record of 13-10 with a 4.50 ERA. Now he's back with the Dodgers, his first team.

Shigetoshi Hasegawa, relief pitcher, Anaheim Angels. Was 5-6 with a 4.04 ERA, pitching 56 innings in 46 games. Now he's with the Mariners.

Tomokazu Ohka, pitcher, Montreal Expos. Was 3-9 with a 5.47 ERA for the Red Sox and Expos.

Masato Yoshii, pitcher, Montreal Expos. Went 4-7 with a 4.78 ERA.

Mac Suzuki, pitcher, Milwaukee Brewers. Was 5-12 with a 5.86 ERA for three teams, the Royals, Rockies and Brewers.

Hideki Irabu, pitcher, Montreal Expos. In three games, the former Yankee was 0-2 with a 4.86 ERA and was released by the Expos in September.

ALBERT PUJOLS
THE GREATEST ROOKIE EVER

In 1911, "Shoeless" Joe Jackson of the Cleveland Indians batted .408 in his rookie season with seven homers and 83 RBIs.

In 1930, Wally Berger of the Boston Braves hit .310 in his rookie season with 38 homers and 119 RBIs.

In 1939, Ted Williams of the Boston Red Sox hit .327 in his rookie season with 31 homers and 145 RBIs.

In 1956, Frank Robinson of the Cincinnati Redlegs hit .290 in his rookie season with 38 homers and 83 RBIs.

And in 1987, Mark McGwire of the Oakland A's hit .289 in his rookie season with 49 homers and 118 RBIs.

These players, all greats, had set the benchmark for Major League rookies.

But Albert Pujols of the St. Louis Cardinals bested them all in 2001.

He didn't have a higher batting average than "Shoeless" Joe's. He didn't hit more homers than McGwire. But Pujols, 21, put it all together in a rookie season for the ages. He batted .329 with 37 homers and set the rookie record for RBIs (130), extra-base hits

(88) and total bases (360). Only one rookie, Hal Trotsky of the 1934 Cleveland Indians, has hit 35 home runs while batting better than .320. He was just the fourth rookie in major league history to hit .300 with 30 homers, 100 RBIs and 100 runs scored, but in overall performance, he was better than any rookie ever.

And he did it while playing four different positions.

"I've had many great players have MVP-caliber seasons," Cardinals manager Tony LaRussa said. "Carlton Fisk, Harold Baines, Jose Canseco, Mark McGwire, Rickey Henderson. But what this kid has done is the greatest performance of any position player I've ever seen."

Added Pirates manager Lloyd McClendon: "I've never seen anything like it. He's quick to the ball with his bat, he hits to all fields, he rarely goes outside the strike zone and no situation seems to rattle him. This young man has a chance to be quite a force for some time in this league."

And Cardinals second baseman Fernando Vina, struggling to put Pujol's season in perspective, gushed, "He's a freak. You don't walk into baseball and do what he's done."

He was the unanimous choice for National League Rookie of the Year, earning all 32 votes and finished fourth in the Most Valuable Player voting behind Barry Bonds, Sammy Sosa and Luis Gonzales. Pujols finished only 56 votes behind Sosa.

And to think: a year ago you would have been in the vast majority if you had asked, "Albert who?"

Pujols was born January 16, 1980, in Santo Domingo, Dominican Republic, and grew up poor. At age 16, he moved with his father to Independence, Missouri, and became a high school star while still learning English. Two years later, he began attending little Maple Woods Community College in Kansas City. As baseball prospects go, he was hardly a blip on the map. But he got better and better, and in 1999, after an outstanding junior college season, Pujols was picked by the Cardinals in the thirteenth round of the amateur draft.

Pujols was signed too late to play that season and began his pro career in 2000 at Class-A Peoria of the Midwest League. He didn't exactly make a smashing first impression. In the team's home opener, playing in front of 1,620 fans, Pujols went hitless in three at-bats. But he got his game into high gear in a hurry and became a minor league sensation, hitting .324 with 17 homers, 84 RBIs and 32 doubles in 109 games, prompting the Cardinals to trade third baseman Fernando Tatis to the Expos over the winter.

"He's a big, strong guy," Cardinals director of player development Mike Jorgensen said. "One of his real strengths is that he doesn't strikeout very much. He has some pop in his bat, he's got some power and he can hit some homeruns. That's pretty remarkable. and I think that's why he's able to hit for average, plus he can use the whole field. He hits the ball in the gaps."

Said Pujols: "As a hitter, I don't try to do too much. I just try to go out there and see the ball and hit the ball. I watch the pitcher and his timing and then go out there and have fun while at the same time trying to get my hits."

During the 2000 season, Pujols was promoted from low-A to high-A to AAA Memphis and hit the game-winning home run in the thirteenth inning of the final game of the Pacific Coast League Championship series to earn series MVP. Then, in the Arizona Fall League, Pujols hit .323 with four homers and 21 RBIs in 27 games. He was on his way . . . to AA ball for the 2001 season. Or so Pujols and the Cardinals organization thought.

He came to the Cardinals' spring training camp in February 2001 as a non-roster player with one year of minor league experience, all but three games of it in Class A. But Pujols quickly showed that he was a special player.

He looked good at third base from the start of training camp, and when LaRussa asked him to play the outfield for a game, Pujols made a diving catch with the bases loaded against Mike Piazza of the Mets. On a day off, Pujols took grounders at shortstop for 50 minutes and so impressed LaRussa with his work ethic that, the next day, he started at short. On the first ball hit to him, he started a double play.

A few days before the season opener, LaRussa told Pujols he had made the team. "But he told me it might just be for the opening

St. Louis fans give Cardinals rookie outfielder Albert Pujols a standing ovation during his at-bat in the seventh inning against the Milwaukee Brewers on September 19. Earlier in the game, Pujols had three RBIs to bring his season total to 120 and break the National League record.

ONE FOR THE AGES: THE PLAYERS

series in Colorado," Pujols said. "He didn't know if I would stay after that."

LaRussa wasn't sure whether he was being sensible by throwing a 21-year-old with one year of pro experience onto the Major League roster, and things didn't look so good at first. Pujols had only one hit in nine at-bats against the Rockies. But when the Cards went to Arizona, Pujols heated up. In the first two games of the series against the Diamondbacks, Pujols had five hits in nine at-bats and his first Major League homer. In the series finale, Pujols walloped a double off the wall against Randy Johnson. By the time the Cardinals flew to St. Louis for their home opener, Pujols was hitting .348. And he never slowed down.

Meanwhile, the Cards were in trouble. McGwire was recovering from knee surgery. Centerfielder Jim Edmonds and shortstop Edgar Renteria were struggling. The veterans were bogging down the team. And on April 15, Pujols had three hits against the Rockies to lift his average to .429. Pujols kept working quietly and hitting loudly. His fielding was more than adequate. Before long, he was batting cleanup.

"Putting a rookie there is not what you want to do," LaRussa said. "I think that's what has been hard, that he's hit in the middle of the lineup and pitchers have been concentrating on him from the first month of the season. And he still has great at-bats. We did it because we had to. There wasn't anybody else."

Said Pujols: "I just went to spring training, tried to do my best, get ready and work hard. They gave me a lot of opportunity to make the club and they gave me a lot of chance to prove what I can do. I always dreamt about this and my dream has come true so far. I'm right here and I'm going to do the best I can."

Pujols hit .370 in April with eight homers and 27 RBIs. In May, he batted .333 with eight homers and 24 RBIs.

"I believe he's been reincarnated, that he played before, in the '20s and '30s, and he's back to prove something," McGwire said. "He fits every definition of what the MVP should be. If we didn't have him, well, I don't want to think where we'd be."

And when the going got tough, Pujols got going. The Cardinals were 54-52 and seven and a half games out of first place in early August when Pujols led them on an eleven-game winning streak that carried them to the National League wildcard. Until late in the season, only once did Pujols play three straight games without a hit, and only once did he play a series without a hit. He batted .360 from August 1 on. Perhaps his most memorable at-bat came on September 21 in Pittsburgh. The Cardinals had blown a 4-0 lead against the Pirates and the game was tied at five with the bases loaded in the top of the ninth.

"I thought, 'We've put such a load on him all year, this is the situation for a double-play ball,'" LaRussa said. "There's not a great chance to get the run home."

But on the third pitch from Omar Olivares, Pujols hit a grand slam for the Cards' eighth straight win. It was his second five RBI night in four days, and LaRussa was using words like "incredible" and "obscene" to describe Pujols's season.

"Everything about Albert is legitimate," La Russa said. "He could do this for a long time. The two biggest issues that could get in the way of him having a great career are, first, that he's a big guy [6'3", 210 pounds]. We saw in spring training that he had stayed in shape. He was quick. The older you get, the tougher it is to carry weight. So he will have to keep up that kind of work. And second, maybe most important, is the atmosphere today in the Major Leagues that if a guy is successful, even if he is just a little successful, much less incredibly successful, he will face a lot of pressure. That might come from his representatives, his family, his friends, his peers. They will say, 'If you have this kind of year, you will make this kind of money.' But he's been so special in so many ways."

Most of all, he impressed people with his humility. He never complained about being moved from one position to the next. He never complained about the pressure of being the Cardinals' key hitter, even though he was only a rookie.

"I want to be in the lineup every day," Pujols said. "Playing anywhere is better than playing the bench. I do what I need to do to stay up here. I don't try to think about records. I don't think about what Ted Williams did or what Frank Robinson did. I'm not trying

ALBERT PUJOLS CAREER STATISTICS

- Height: 6'3"
- Weight: 210 lbs.
- Throws: Right
- Bats: Right
- Born: January 16, 1980, Santo Domingo, Dominican Republic

SEASON	TEAM	G	AB	R	H	2B	3B	HR	RBI	BB	SO	SB	CS	OBP	SLG	OPS	AVG
2001	ST. LOUIS	161	590	112	194	47	4	37	130	69	93	1	3	.403	.610	1.013	.329

to have a great year as a rookie setting records. I am trying to get my baseball team into the playoffs and World Series. That is the only record that I want. I shouldn't be tired from playing baseball. I don't go out and drink and do a lot of things. I spend time with my family. That's my hobby. That's it. Family and baseball."

He did get the Cardinals into the post-season, and his two-run homer off Randy Johnson in Game Two of the Divisional Series helped St. Louis tie the series at one. The Cardinals lost in five (Pujols was hitless in the last three games), but that couldn't erase his amazing season. He was the fifth rookie to lead the Cardinals in batting average, the first since Bake McBride in 1974. He was the seventh rookie to lead the team in homers, the first since Todd Zeile in 1990. He was the third to lead the team in RBIs, the first since Joe Medwick in 1933. The only other rookie to lead the club in all three categories was Rogers Hornsby, in 1916. Pujols was the first player in Cardinals history to take the team's "Triple Crown"— batting average, homers, RBIs— since Ted Simmons did it in 1973. And he was almost as good in August and September as he was in April and May.

"We had a year out of Albert Pujols that I don't know if it'll ever be repeated during my time here from a rookie," Cardinals General Manager Walt Jocketty said.

It might never be repeated ever.

ROGER CLEMENS
THE ROCKET MAN ROCKETS TO VICTORY

FIVE YEARS AGO, after Roger Clemens finished the 1996 season with a record of 10-13, the Red Sox decided that The Rocket Man was in the "twilight of his career" and decided to let him leave Boston. In 2001, Clemens proved that he wasn't in the twilight of anything. He was still in the limelight.

It was an incredible season for Clemens, who turned 39 on August 4, 2001. On Opening Day, he passed Walter "Big Train" Johnson as the American League's all-time strikeout leader. He started the season in eighth place on the all-time strikeout list and finished in third. He compiled a 20-3 record to win his sixth Cy Young Award.

And he won 16 straight games.

Game-by-game, it was a season to remember.

1-0. April 2, New York: Clemens not only went eight and one-third innings, allowing seven hits and striking out five in a 7-3 win over the Kansas City Royals. He also broke Johnson's record for career strikeouts and left to a standing ovation from the sellout crowd in the ninth inning.

Clemens tied the record in the eighth inning when he struckout

Carlos Beltran swinging and walked out to the mound for the ninth inning to a loud ovation. He then struckout Joe Randa for the first out of the inning for his 3,509th career K, eclipsing the Big Train's mark. The Yankees rushed out of the dugout to congratulate Clemens, who was then removed from the game by manager Joe Torre.

"On my way in, I talked to my mother in Houston," Clemens said. "She was having a good day and, in turn, I felt good. She said, 'Son, you're very blessed. It's another feather in your cap, so enjoy it.' My mom enjoys the history of the game as much as I do. I'll think about it the rest of the day.

"Once I tied the record, I desperately wanted to do it here. It was great."

2-0. April 8, New York: Clemens struggled, allowing five runs on eight hits, but the Yankees gave him plenty of support in a 16-5 win over Toronto at Yankee Stadium. He had a 12-0 lead before allowing all five runs in the fourth inning.

"Roger had some real good stuff," Torre said. "Early on, that was vintage Roger. I think those long innings caught up with him, but he came back and really settled in and threw goose eggs."

Said Clemens, "I had nice velocity to start with, but I had a little trouble gripping the ball. For the most part, I was able to do what I wanted to today."

3-0. April 29, New York: After getting no decision in three straight starts, a 3-2 victory over Boston, an extra-innings Yankees win over Toronto, and a loss to Seattle in which he pitched poorly, Clemens picked up his third win in a 3-1 victory over Oakland and moved into sixth place on the all-time strikeout list.

Clemens got Miguel Tejada looking on a 2-2 curveball in the seventh inning for his 3,534th career strikeout, tying Gaylord Perry for sixth place. Then he got the next batter, Jeremy Giambi, looking to pass Perry.

"It's a pleasure," Clemens said. "Gaylord is one of the great names of the past. To have it happen here, at home, on a good afternoon, I was able to enjoy it for just a second before I got locked back in. At this stage of my career, I'm very fortunate."

The achievement came on the fifteenth anniversary of the date that Clemens set a Major League record by striking out 20 Seattle Mariners.

4-0. May 9, New York: Clemens was trailing, 5-3, when he left the May 4 game against the Orioles in the sixth inning, but the Yankees rallied to save him from the loss. Five days later, he pitched his best game of the season, going eight innings and allowing only four hits in a 2-0 win over the Minnesota Twins.

4-1. May 20, Seattle: In what would be Clemens's only loss until late September, he allowed five runs in seven innings and lost to the red-hot Seattle Mariners, 6-2. And then the fun started.

5-1. May 26, Cleveland: Clemens struggled early and allowed five runs, but the Yankees beat the Indians. Yet, even on a day when he didn't have his best stuff, he moved into fifth place on the career strikeout list.

"I could have been gone after the fourth inning," Clemens said. "I don't think I had a whole lot. It was a battle."

Clemens passed Don Sutton on the list when he struckout Jacob Cruz in the seventh inning for career K No. 3,575. Only Tom Seaver (3,640), Bert Blyleven (3,701), Steve Carlton (4,136) and Nolan Ryan were ahead of him.

"It's longevity," Clemens said. "Being able to have your name mentioned with those guys is very gratifying. It's pretty neat and gives me an appreciation of what they've all done."

"The thing that I like most is that he didn't have his best stuff and he still battled," Torre said. "He's had a pretty incredible career."

And he was on his way to a pretty incredible season.

6-1. June 2, New York: Clemens struggled again, but his team gave him plenty of run support in a 9-4 win over the Indians at Yankee Stadium. He struckout six and allowed nine hits and four runs in six innings. The only drama came in the sixth inning, when Clemens grabbed the back of his leg and limped around the mound.

"Once I saw him limping around, I feared the worst," Torre said. But it was just a leg cramp and Clemens stayed in to retire one more batter.

"I felt my leg buckle under me and I felt it cramp," Clemens said. "When I got up and straightened it out, it was better."

7-1. June 7, New York: This time, Clemens had his best stuff. He allowed only three hits and struckout ten in eight innings as the Yankees beat the Orioles, 4-0, at Yankee Stadium. Clemens's 267th victory moved him ahead of Hall of Famers Bob Feller and Eppa Rixey and into 30th place on the career wins list.

"That was the best stuff I've ever seen him throw," Baltimore's Jerry Hairston said. "When he has the split-finger working, he's tough to beat."

8-1. June 13, New York: Clemens again pitched strongly, allowing three runs and seven hits in eight innings as the Yankees beat Montreal, 9-3. Clemens allowed all three runs in the first and second innings before settling down.

"Roger is one of those guys who gets stronger as the game goes on," Expos manager Jeff Torborg said. "Just like Nolan Ryan used to. When you score against him you better keep going."

9-1. June 18, Detroit: Another big-time outing. Seven innings, no earned runs, in a 10-1 win over the Tigers at Comerica Park. He allowed his only run in the first inning. His 269th career victory moved him past Jim Palmer and into 29th place on the all-time list.

10-1. June 23, St. Petersburg, Florida: More vintage Clemens. Eight strikeouts and only one run allowed in six innings as the Yankees beat the Devil Rays, 2-1. The Yankees scored a run in the seventh to break a 1-1 tie, then Clemens got help from reliever Mike Stanton in the seventh. He left the game with runners at first and third and no outs, but Stanton worked out of the jam.

11-1. June 29, New York: Back home, Clemens pitched shutout ball for six innings, tired in the seventh and beat the Devil Rays, 7-5.

"This is the guy we traded for," Torre said. "He's obviously having an All-Star year."

Clemens's 271st career win moved him into a tie for 28th on the all-time list.

12-1. July 4, Baltimore. On a steamy hot day, Clemens lasted and beat the Orioles, 4-3.

"It was so hot, I had to readjust my sights," Clemens said. "I just wanted to try and outlast the other guy."

"We expect him to win just about every time he takes the mound," said Torre, who earlier in the day selected him to the American League All-Star team. "For the last year, he's gone out there with good stuff just about every time."

"I'm just trying to ride the momentum every time I go out there," Clemens said.

13-1. July 18, Detroit: The Yankees had a problem. About 90 minutes before game time, the Yankees were looking for a starting pitcher because Adrian Hernandez was sick. Clemens volunteered to start on three days rest.

"I'll remember this because of the situation we were in and the way he went about it," Yankees pitching coach Mel Stottlemyre said.

Clemens, pitching on three days rest for the first time since 1993, gave up five runs in five and two-thirds innings and was saved when the Yankees scored three runs in the sixth and two in the seventh for an 8-5 win.

Maybe Clemens owed his teammates one: in his previous start against Florida, he left the game trailing 3-2, but the Yankees rallied to win and save his streak.

14-1. July 23, New York: The Rocket Man moved ahead of Hall of Famer Tom Seaver and into fourth place on the career strikeouts list with his tenth straight win, 7-2 over the Toronto Blue Jays at Yankee Stadium. He got Luis Lopez looking in the fifth inning for his 3,641st career K.

"It's OK," Lopez said. "There are some 4,000-some odd guys with me."

"Tom Seaver is just a tremendous name and a tremendous pitcher and a tremendous person," Clemens said. "He was a teammate, and in the short time he was, I was able to learn a lot from him. Doing it here in front of this crowd in this uniform with so much tradition really makes it special."

His 274th career victory also moved him ahead of Red Ruffing for 27th on the all-time list.

15-1. July 28, Toronto: Anyone could have won this one. The Yankees scored big and Clemens allowed only one hit and struckout eight over five and two-thirds innings of a 12-1 victory over the Blue

Roger Clemens was the most dominant pitcher in the American League during the 2001 season. In addition to breaking the all-time American League career strikeout record, he also won 16 straight games and his record sixth Cy Young Award.

Jays. But Clemens provided his team with a scare. He left the game in the sixth inning with cramps in his right groin.

"I know it's not as severe as I've done it in the past, so I don't expect it to linger," Clemens said. "I knew that something wasn't right. When I kicked the dirt I felt it a little more, so at that point I knew my legs were trying to shut down. I use my legs a great deal. I'll get treatment, and cut back on some of the things I'll do."

16-1. August 15, New York: Clemens didn't miss a start, but he was dealt two straight no decisions that turned into Yankees wins. Then he beat the Blue Jays, 10-3 at Yankee Stadium, for his twelfth straight victory, making him the first Major League pitcher in thirty-two years to have a record of 16-1, when Dave McNally did it for the 1969 Baltimore Orioles.

"I don't know the history behind it, and I don't think it matters unless we get to where we want to be: staying in first place and reaching our goals," Clemens said after he helped the Yankees do just that. "It makes all the work I do seem to pay off."

"He certainly has been leading this staff all year," Torre said. "He hasn't had a bad start yet."

17-1. August 25, Anaheim: First, the Yankees bailed out Clemens. On August 20, Clemens struggled and was trailing 5-2 after five innings. The Yankees trailed, 5-4, when Clemens left the game after the sixth, but rallied to win, 9-5.

Then, five days later, Clemens made it thirteen straight with a 7-5 win over the Angels in Anaheim. Clemens pitched seven innings and allowed only two runs, making him the first American League pitcher ever to win 17 of his first 18 decisions in a season.

"He's going to be in the record book a lot, and this is another notch for him," Torre said. "He's remarkable. He's 39 years old and has the body of a 30-year-old. He's won five Cy Youngs and he's not living off it. He's out there trying to better it."

18-1. August 31, Boston: Clemens completed the month with a gem, a 3-1 victory over his old team, the Red Sox, in front of a loud, surly crowd at Fenway Park. The Yankees trailed, 1-0, after the seventh inning, but scored two in the eighth and one in the ninth. Clemens deserved the win: he walked none and struckout ten in a vintage outing.

Jorge Posada hit a two-run homer in the eighth to give the Yankees the lead, and the bullpen shut down the Sox the rest of the way.

The key moments came early in the game. Boston had runners in scoring position in the second, third and fourth innings, but Clemens wouldn't let them score. They had runners on first and third with one out in the sixth, but Clemens got the last two batters.

"When he got out of the first-and-third jam that was huge for us," Torre said. "That kept us in the ballgame and gave us a little pop of energy."

19-1. September 5, Toronto: More records. Clemens set the Yankees record with his fifteenth straight win, 4-3, over the Blue Jays. When the game ended, Torre handed Clemens the lineup card.

"It's special," Clemens said. "It's nice to have the lineup card. Skip handed it to me as soon as he walked through the door, and Mariano Rivera handed me the baseball. Those will be treasured, and I definitely will be able to look at those in the offseason and know what they mean."

Clemens passed Jack Chesbro and Whitey Ford on the Yankees list.

"Rocket is remarkable," Torre said. "Nineteen and one is one thing, 39 years old is another thing. To still be the power pitcher, the dominant pitcher that he is, is remarkable, and yet when you watch on a day-to-day basis, you can understand why he is successful."

20-1. September 19, Chicago: After the September 11 tragedy, Clemens walked into Comiskey Park and beat the White Sox, 6-3, to clinch his sixth 20-win season and third since leaving Boston. But afterwards, Clemens was in no mood to celebrate.

"It just doesn't take on as much meaning as it would have because of the circumstances," Clemens said after he became the first pitcher in Major League history to go 20-1. "It's a different feeling. There are a lot of things we take for granted, and I didn't know how I'd feel once I got out on the mound. It's a special win and maybe some time down the road I'll take the time to reflect on its meaning. I've been around for a long time and to win twenty games at this stage of my career is definitely a blessing."

Clemens became the American League's oldest 20-game winner since Early Wynn won twenty in 1959.

ROGER CLEMENS CAREER STATISTICS

- Height: 6'4"
- Weight: 238 lbs.
- Throws: Right
- Bats: Right
- Born: August 4, 1962, Dayton, Ohio

SEASON	TEAM	G	GS	CG	SHO	IP	H	R	ER	HR	BB	SO	W	L	SV	HLD	BLSV	ERA
1984	BOSTON	21	20	5	1	133.1	146	67	64	13	29	126	9	4	0	0	0	4.32
1985	BOSTON	15	15	3	1	98.1	83	38	36	5	37	74	7	5	0	0	0	3.30
1986	BOSTON	33	33	10	1	254.0	179	77	70	21	67	238	24	4	0	0	0	2.48
1987	BOSTON	36	36	18	7	281.2	248	100	93	19	83	256	20	9	0	0	0	2.97
1988	BOSTON	35	35	14	8	264.0	217	93	86	17	62	291	18	12	0	0	0	2.93
1989	BOSTON	35	35	8	3	253.1	215	101	88	20	93	230	17	11	0	0	0	3.13
1990	BOSTON	31	31	7	4	228.1	193	59	49	7	54	209	21	6	0	0	0	1.93
1991	BOSTON	35	35	13	4	271.1	219	93	79	15	65	241	18	10	0	0	0	2.62
1992	BOSTON	32	32	11	5	246.2	203	80	66	11	62	208	18	11	0	0	0	2.41
1993	BOSTON	29	29	2	1	191.2	175	99	95	17	67	160	11	14	0	0	0	4.46
1994	BOSTON	24	24	3	1	170.2	124	62	54	15	71	168	9	7	0	0	0	2.85
1995	BOSTON	23	23	0	0	140.0	141	70	65	15	60	132	10	5	0	0	0	4.18
1996	BOSTON	34	34	6	2	242.2	216	106	98	19	106	257	10	13	0	0	0	3.64
1997	TORONTO	34	34	9	3	264.0	204	65	60	9	68	292	21	7	0	0	0	2.04
1998	TORONTO	33	33	5	3	234.2	169	78	69	11	88	271	20	6	0	0	0	2.65
1999	YANKEES	30	30	1	1	187.2	185	101	96	20	90	163	14	10	0	0	0	4.60
2000	YANKEES	32	32	1	0	204.1	184	96	84	26	84	188	13	8	0	0	0	3.70
2001	YANKEES	33	33	0	0	220.1	205	94	86	19	72	213	20	3	0	0	0	3.51
CAREER TOTALS		545	544	116	45	3887.0	3306	1479	1338	279	1258	3717	280	145	0	0	0	3.10

But the streak ended there. On September 25, the Blue Jays shut out Clemens and the Yankees, 4-0, at Yankee Stadium. Clemens pitched six and two-thirds innings and allowed four runs as his 16-game winning streak was snapped. On a night when baseball returned to Yankee Stadium for the first time since the terrorist attacks, the Yankees clinched the division title despite losing, and Clemens moved past Bert Blyleven and into third place on the all-time strikeout list with his 3,702nd K.

"The game was secondary to what went on," Clemens said.

Clemens also lost his final start of the season to finish 20-3. He would win only one game in the post-season as the Yankees failed to capture their fourth straight World Series. In Game Seven of the World

Series, Clemens allowed only one run in six-plus innings, but the Yankees lost to the Arizona Diamondbacks. But in November, Clemens added to one more record: He overwhelmingly was awarded his sixth American League Cy Young Award. No other pitcher in either league has ever won more than four. He was the only pitcher named on all twenty-eight ballots.

"Once the streak got over ten games, you start hearing about it and seeing it, and you get into a mode where you just don't feel like you're going to lose," Clemens said. "But to me, the Cy Young is a team award, also. Those guys make me shine, make me look good when I'm out there on the mound. Every time I look at a Cy Young Award, I thnk of the guys who were behind me that helped me win it.

"They're all special. My first one was very new to me, everything that went on around it. This one, I take some of the memories and the history that goes along with it. I'll remember this one for those reasons."

Clemens had one of the most successful seasons by any pitcher in baseball history. He did it at age 39. Just imagine what he'll do at age 40.

SAMMY SOSA
SWINGING SAMMY SWINGS TO 60 AGAIN

Mark McGwire smashed Roger Maris's single-season homerun record to pieces in 1998 when he hit 70 homers. Barry Bonds made mincemeat out of McGwire's record in the 2001 season when he hit 73 homeruns. These are the players who have held the Major League records for hitting homeruns, but over the past four seasons, nobody has hit the ball out of the park consistently like Sammy Sosa of the Chicago Cubs.

In 2001, Sosa hit 64 homeruns, making him the first player in history to hit 60 or more homers in three seasons.

Sosa's numbers over the past four seasons are incredible. Power-wise, he has recorded the most prolific four-season stretch in Major League history: 243 homeruns, 597 runs batted in, 500 runs scored and 367 extra-base hits. He has homered at least 50 times in each of the last four seasons and has homered over 60 times in three of the past four seasons. Mark McGwire and Babe Ruth are the only other players with more than two 50-homer seasons. In fact, Sosa now holds three of the top six spots for single-season homeruns.

He never set the single-season homerun record, but Sammy Sosa is the only player in Major League history to have three seasons with 60 or more homers. Here's Sosa connecting for his 60th off Cincinnati Reds pitcher Lance Davis on October 2 at Wrigley Field in Chicago.

And he's done all of this while proving that life begins at 30. Sosa, 34, had only 207 homers from 1989 to 1997 and was a career .257 hitter.

Sosa has become a hero in a town that worships its athletes. When all is said and done, Sosa will be mentioned in the same breath as Chicago sports heroes Ernie Banks, Michael Jordan, George Halas and Bobby Hull. The bleacher bums bow to him when he runs out to rightfield at the start of each home game at Wrigley Field. And his homeruns are impressive not only because of how many he hits, but because of how far he hits them. Far. Very far. And, while fellow homerun hitters Barry Bonds and McGwire are perceived as moody and aloof, Sosa is a player fans and teammates alike adore.

"What surprised me after being around him for two years how intense he is," Cubs shortstop Ricky Gutierrez said. "He takes every at-bat seriously. You rarely see him give an at-bat away no matter what the score is or how many hits he has or how many homeruns he has. It's like every at-bat is his last one."

Said Cubs pitcher Kevin Tapani: "What amazes me is how disciplined he's gotten at the plate. It's a huge change from where he was because he was a dead hacker the way he was swinging. To make that type of transition after six or seven years in the big leagues is impressive."

Added Cubs second baseman Eric Young: "What really surprised me was how he goes about his business and enjoys the game every day. He hustles out to the field and enjoys himself each and every day. I've seen big swingers who wake up, don't take batting practice and hit very well. Sammy really works hard each and every day. I could see him taking a day or two off, but I can't remember him taking a day off."

A cynic could try to downgrade Sosa's accomplishments over the past four seasons. After all, he didn't hit his 100th career homer until his sixth Major League season. Sosa has apparently taken advantage of the downturn in the quality of pitching. Yet, even if that's so, no batter has taken advantage like Sosa has. In an era of diminished pitching, Sosa has made pitchers seem even more diminished.

"I think it's pretty difficult no matter where you play or when you do it," Houston Astros power hitter Jeff Bagwell said. "In this day and time of specialty pitchers and all that kind of stuff, to go out and hit 400 homeruns is a tremendous accomplishment. I don't care when you did it. I'm sure back in 1978, they were saying it's not as great an accomplishment as it was in the '40s. To me, it's an amazing accomplishment.

Sosa entered the 2001 season with 386 homers. He was homerless in his first four games, then went on a tear and carried the surprising Cubs with him. When he slumped in late April and May, the Cubbies slumped with him. Yet, Sosa found time to reach a milestone on May 16 at Wrigley Field. In the bottom of the fourth inning, Sosa swung at a two balls, one strike pitch from Houston's Shane Reynolds and deposited the ball into the rightfield bleachers for his 400th career homerun. The homer moved Sosa into 33rd place on the all-time homerun list, ahead of Al Kaline. He became the seventh Cub to reach 400, joining Jimmie Foxx, Ernie Banks, Dave Kingman, Andre Dawson, Billy Williams and Rafael Palmeiro.

"It's something that, as a person and a player, you want to get to," Sosa said of 400. "I've got to continue."

Banks, the Cubs' all-time career homerun leader, was overjoyed as he watched Sosa's blast sail out of the park.

"When he gets on the field, he reminds me of Tiger Woods because he's so focused on what he has to do," Banks said.

Sosa found himself at the center of a joyous summer in Chicago. The Cubs battled for the National League Central pennant with Houston and St. Louis, so each Sosa homer actually meant something besides another mark on his personal ledger. When Sosa homered twice in a 5-4 victory over the Astros on July 21, the 50th multi-homer game of his career, Chicago moved 16 games over .500 and three games ahead of Houston in the NL Central.

"We are a team. I don't do it all myself," Sosa said. "We really have one thing on our minds and that's to finish first. We've got a great club and we know that we can compete with anybody."

The Cubs still had high hopes even after Sosa homered three times in a 14-5 loss to Colorado on August 9 at Wrigley Field. He might have hit four had Cubs manager Don Baylor, in a concession to the heat and a nine-run deficit, not replaced him after the seventh inning. After hitting his 40th homer in the seventh inning, Sosa acknowledged the cheers of the crowd of 38,345 and took a brief curtain call at the top of the dugout steps. He joined Hall of Famer Ernie Banks as the only Cubs with five 40-homer seasons.

Sosa had a spectacular second half. He hit only 15 homers in April and May, putting him way behind league leader Barry Bonds, but made a race of the homerun derby with 17 in August. He had another three-homer game against Milwaukee on August 22, and powered into baseball history with two homers against the Cardinals on August 26. His 50th and 51st homers of the season allowed him to join McGwire and Ruth as the only Major League players with four 50-homer seasons.

"I'm not going to lie to you. I am very happy to be in that category with Mr. Mark McGwire and Babe," Sosa said. "I still got to continue. I'm not satisfied right now, the season is not over yet and we have a mission to finish in first."

In the first inning, Sosa sent a three-two pitch from Dustin Hermanson into the right-centerfield bleachers for No. 50, a two-run shot that set off a loud ovation at Wrigley Field. Sosa added a solo shot off Hermanson in the fifth, a high drive that landed in the shrubbery in centerfield. The crowd of 39,045 at Wrigley cheered until Sosa emerged from the dugout, doffed his cap and took curtain calls after both of his homers.

One of Sosa's most impressive homers came in a 5-3 victory over the Braves on September 1 at Turner Field in Atlanta. His two-run homer off pitcher Greg Maddux in the first inning traveled an estimated 471 feet, making it the longest homer in the five-year history of Turner Field.

"I've never seen a homerun hit so far," teammate Julian Tavarez said. "I was thinking, 'That had to be at least 600 feet.'"

The Braves didn't take any chances Sosa's next two times up. They intentionally walked him both times.

The season ended on a down note for Sosa and the Cubs. Chicago lost five of six games before the September 11 tragedy, then lost five of eight games when the season continued and slowly dropped out of the pennant race and the wild-card chase. On October 2, the same day that Sosa hit his 60th homer of the season, the Cubs lost to Cincinnati, 5-4, and officially dropped out of the playoff chase.

It was a bittersweet night. Sosa deserved to have a smile on his face after the game, but the Cubs blew a three-run lead and lost in the ninth inning. So, after the game, smiling Sammy wasn't smiling. He was lamenting what could have been. The playoffs were out of reach, and Bonds was out of reach, too.

Yet, the fans at Wrigley Field refused to not enjoy Sosa. They cheered when he stepped to the plate in the first inning and booed when Reds pitcher Lance Davis threw three consecutive pitches out of the strike zone. With the count three-one, Sosa swung at a fastball and drove it into the back of the left-centerfield bleachers to become baseball's first three-time 60-homerun hitter.

"It's nice," Sosa said. He had gone 16 at-bats without a homer since hitting No. 59 against the Astros on September 27. "I'm not going to complain about it, but I can't sit back and think about that right now. I was getting a little anxious because everyone in the whole world was waiting for me to hit No. 60. When I was rounding the bases, I was thinking of everything that I've been through. I felt great for my family and my people."

The homerun was significant for several other reasons. His 150th RBI of the season marked the seventh time a player has hit 50 homers and 150 RBIs in a season. Sosa, who also did it in 1998, is the only player to accomplish the feat since World War II. The homer also gave Sosa 98 extra-base hits, breaking Hack Wilson's club record.

"I sometimes ask myself: 'What would happen if every time I hit a homerun we won?'" Sosa said. "We'd be in first place."

Sosa finished the season in style. The Cubs lost their season finale, 4-3, to the Pirates, but Sammy hit his 64th homer in the eighth inning. In typically generous fashion, Sosa dedicated the homerun to Arne Harris, who had produced and directed Cubs telecasts for 38 years and died the night before.

SAMMY SOSA CAREER STATISTICS

- Height: 6'
- Weight: 225 lbs.
- Throws: Right
- Bats: Right
- Born: November 12, 1968, San Pedro de Macoris, Dominican Republic

SEASON	TEAM	G	AB	R	H	2B	3B	HR	RBI	BB	SO	SB	CS	OBP	SLG	OPS	AVG
1989	WHITE SOX	33	99	19	27	5	0	3	10	11	27	7	3	.351	.414	.765	.273
1989	TEXAS	25	84	8	20	3	0	1	3	0	20	0	2	.238	.310	.548	.238
1989	TOTALS	58	183	27	47	8	0	4	13	11	47	7	5	.303	.366	.669	.257
1990	WHITE SOX	153	532	72	124	26	10	15	70	33	150	32	16	.282	.404	.686	.233
1991	WHITE SOX	116	316	39	64	10	1	10	33	14	98	13	6	.240	.335	.575	.203
1992	CUBS	67	262	41	68	7	2	8	25	19	63	15	7	.317	.393	.710	.260
1993	CUBS	159	598	92	156	25	5	33	93	38	135	36	11	.309	.485	.794	.261
1994	CUBS	105	426	59	128	17	6	25	70	25	92	22	13	.339	.545	.884	.300
1995	CUBS	144	564	89	151	17	3	36	119	58	134	34	7	.340	.500	.840	.268
1996	CUBS	124	498	84	136	21	2	40	100	34	134	18	5	.323	.564	.887	.273
1997	CUBS	162	642	90	161	31	4	36	119	45	174	22	12	.300	.480	.780	.251
1998	CUBS	159	643	134	198	20	0	66	158	73	171	18	9	.377	.647	1.024	.308
1999	CUBS	162	625	114	180	24	2	63	141	78	171	7	8	.367	.635	1.002	.288
2000	CUBS	156	604	106	193	38	1	50	138	91	168	7	4	.406	.634	1.040	.320
2001	CUBS	160	577	146	189	34	5	64	160	116	153	0	2	.437	.737	1.174	.328
CAREER	TOTALS	1725	6470	1093	1795	278	41	450	1239	635	1690	231	105	.343	.542	.885	.277

"We had a great relationship," Sosa said. "He always took care of me."

Sosa finished the season with 160 RBIs, the third-highest total in National League history behind Hack Wilson (191) and Chuck Klein (170). Sosa's 425 total bases broke Wilson's 71-year club record. He would finish second in the National League Most Valuable Player balloting, behind Bonds.

In the end, Sosa lamented the Cubs' failure to make the playoffs, but he had nothing to be ashamed of. In every way, he *was* the Cubs. He hit 47 more homers than any other player on the team. He drove in 94 more runs than any other Cub. He hit a career-high .328. He hit 29 homers from August on.

Sammy Sosa has made baseball fun again in Chicago. And he has become the elite homerun hitter of the homerun era.

RANDY JOHNSON
THE BIG UNIT PUTS UP SOME BIG NUMBERS

HE'S UNFAIR. Randy Johnson is six-foot-ten, the tallest pitcher in baseball, and although he weighs only 232 pounds, making him look anything but athletic, he towers over opposing batters—we won't call them hitters, because they're not—as he stands on the mound. The poor souls don't know whether he's going to throw his 99-mile-per-hour fastball or his 89-mile-per-hour slider until it's too late, and then they're left flailing helplessly at empty air.

On top of that, he's a lefty.

On top of that, he has pinpoint control.

On top of that, he plays for the best team in baseball, so he knows he can make an occasional mistake.

"The guy throws 95 to 96, and a split, a slider, a changeup and a curveball," Giants rightfielder Armando Rios said. "You don't know what to look for. You sit on something and pray for a strike. Before he was overpowering. Now he's overpowering and he can play with your head. He keeps you guessing all the time."

In the 2001 season, Arizona Diamondbacks ace Randy Johnson was more unfair than ever, even though he turned 38 in September, an age when most players—no less power pitchers—are thinking about calling it quits. The pitcher known as The Big Unit turned in one of the most spectacular seasons ever by a starting pitcher. He won a career high 21 games, losing only six. His ERA of 2.49 gave him his second ERA title in three years. He was 16-2 over his last 24 games, 12-1 in his last 13 decisions and 10-2 after Arizona losses. He reached 300 strikeouts for the fourth consecutive season, another Major League first. His 372 strikeouts led the league for the eighth time, as well as being the third-highest total ever. And he won his fourth Cy Young Award.

How's this for domination: Since 1995, when he played for the Seattle Mariners, Johnson is 119-39 with a 2.66 ERA and 2,082 strikeouts in 213 games.

And how's this for unfair: Johnson started a one-two punch completed by righty Curt Schilling, who was nearly as dominant with 22 wins and a 2.98 ERA. The two pitched back-to-back 16 times, during which Arizona never lost consecutive games. The Johnson-Schilling tandem drew favorable comparisons to the Dodgers' tandem of Sandy Koufax and Don Drysdale in the 1960s.

"They made forty percent of our starts and were about 140 percent responsible for us getting into the playoffs," Arizona's Mark Grace said.

In an historic season for Johnson, he had two history-making games. The first was on May 8 in Phoenix against the Cincinnati Reds. He became the first lefthander to strike out 20 batters in a game, joining Chicago Cubs righty Kerry Wood and Roger Clemens, who did it twice for the Boston Red Sox.

Johnson struckout two in each of the first three innings and struckout the side in the fourth, giving him nine for the night. When he fanned the leadoff hitter in the fifth, ten of the first thirteen outs had been recorded on strikeouts. Aaron Boone broke up the perfect game, then Johnson K'd Pokey Reese to end the fifth. But Johnson still had only 12 strikeouts after six innings before striking out the side in the seventh and eighth innings.

Johnson mowed down pinch-hitter Deion Sanders on three pitches to open the ninth, retired Donnie Sadler on a grounder to shortstop, then faced Juan Castro in what figured to be his final chance to get No. 20. He worked the count to two-two on Juan Castro, then threw a fastball. Castro swung and missed. Johnson had No. 20. Twice before he had struckout 19 in a game, so when he reached the milestone, Johnson thrust his glove into the air, shouted to the sky, then lifted his hat to the cheering crowd.

"I'd been baffled with my mechanics," said Johnson, who merely had 58 strikeouts in his last five starts. "I remained fairly calm out there, showed no emotion and with me, I show emotion and a lot of adrenaline. I stayed within myself and just had a lot of fun. Of course, getting ahead of the hitters helps a lot."

But the game was tied, and when the D-Backs failed to score in the bottom half of the inning, Arizona manager Bob Brenly decided to go to his bullpen. So, Johnson was denied the record for most strikeouts in a nine-inning game because the game went into extra innings.

"No point going out there for the tenth inning," Johnson said. "I surely could have gone out, but what was the point? It's important for me to go out for my next start."

"I just said to him, 'How're you doing?'" Brenly said, "and by the look on his face and the exhale of breath when I asked him that question, I thought he had enough. He was physically and mentally spent. He gave everything he had. There's a reason we have a bullpen. I know it was an extraordinary performance but in my judgment, we had gotten the last out from him."

Maybe, although Johnson had achieved eight of his last nine outs on strikeouts.

"It's much like a no-hitter," Johnson said. "If it happens, it was meant to be. If it doesn't happen, well, you just say you still gave it all you had. There are only two other players in the history of baseball who have done it. There's a great deal of satisfaction in doing it."

The record for most strikeouts in a game is 21, set by Tom Cheney, who pitched every inning of a 16-inning game for the Washington Senators in 1962. Johnson's record will be listed as second under most strikeouts in an extra-inning game, but he won't be listed as the co-holder of the record for strikeouts in a nine-inning game. That was of little concern to Johnson, who felt his accomplishment equaled Clemens's and Wood's.

"When someone says I don't hold the record, well I did what they did in nine," Johnson said. "I'm not losing sleep over it. I know what I did."

In all, Johnson threw 124 pitches, 92 for strikes, and walked none. He struckout the side three times and struckout two in five other innings. He allowed only three hits.

"When guys like him get going, you could just put your glove on your head because they're not going to hit the ball," Grace said. "Just an awesome display of power pitching."

There were many other games during the 2001 season when Johnson's teammates could have left their gloves home. In three straight starts on June 3, 8 and 14 against San Diego, Kansas City and the Cubs, Johnson K'd 14, 11 and 11 respectively. In three straight appearances on July 18, 24 and 29, he fanned 16, 14 and 12 respectively. Forget about one-game or two-game grooves. Johnson was on a season-long run.

Johnson didn't even start his second history-making game, which began on the evening of July 18th and ended on the afternoon of the 19th. Schilling started the game against the San Diego Padres and pitched two perfect innings. But then, in the top of the third inning, with the D-Backs leading 1-0, two electrical explosions knocked out the lights in leftfield, forcing the game to be suspended.

Johnson was supposed to start the next day's regularly scheduled game, but Brenly looked over the Padres' lineup for the continuation game and came up with a plan: the Padres' lineup was loaded with lefthanded hitters to face the righty Schilling. There was no way Schilling could pitch again after warming up and pitching the night before. If moved up to start the continued game, the lefty Johnson could dominate the Padres.

Of course, he probably could've dominated them anyway, but what happened was a total mismatch. Making only his tenth relief appearance of his career—and his only one of the season—Johnson, staked to a 1-0 lead, struckout 16, the Major League record for a reliever, and came within four outs of a no-hitter in a 3-0 win for

Randy Johnson had one of the most dominant seasons by a pitcher ever.

Arizona. Wiki Gonzalez hit an opposite-field single to right on the first pitch he saw from Johnson with two outs in the eighth for the Padres' only hit. Johnson broke the record held by Washington Senators pitcher Walter Johnson, who K'd 15 in 11-1/3 innings of relief work in a 15-inning game in July 1913.

"He might be the best long man in baseball, huh?" Brenly joked. "That was stellar Randy Johnson right there. He had great command. When he needed to throw the slider, he had that in his back pocket. He had great command. He had a real good rhythm. I wish he could start the second game."

The Padres fared no better against Johnson as a starter. In his next outing against San Diego, just a week later, he fanned 14.

In what would turn out to be an emotional, suspenseful season for the Diamondbacks, an expansion team in only their fourth season, Johnson supplied very little suspense. And there was no countdown to his 300th strikeout. No question about whether or not he'd reach the mark. Johnson didn't have to wait until the final game of the season, or even the final month. He got the milestone K on August 23 in a 5-1 loss to the Pirates in Pittsburgh—his first loss since late June. He left the game after seven innings with 303 strikeouts for the season, moving him past Phil Niekro for ninth place on the all-time list with 3,343 strikeouts. He struckout the side on nine pitches in the sixth inning to tie a Major League record for efficiency shared by 31 other pitchers. The last strikeout in the sixth, of rookie Jack Wilson swinging, was Johnson's 300th of the season.

With No. 300 out of the way, Johnson gave chase to Ryan's Major League record of 383 strikeouts in a season. On September 27 against Milwaukee at Bank One Ballpark in Phoenix, Johnson struckout 16 batters in six and two-thirds innings to become a 20-game winner for the second time in his career, tie the Major League record he shared with Ryan for 23 double-digit strikeouts in a season and move 17 strikeouts short of Ryan's single-season record. Johnson was scheduled to start two more games, but he said he would not pitch in the regular season finale at Milwaukee if Arizona had already clinched the division title.

But Johnson's season was already more impressive than Ryan's record-breaking season. He had pitched eighty fewer innings than Ryan.

"If the innings were there, I would assume it would be something I could possibly break," Johnson said. "It's truly not that important to me. When you get that close, you would like to do it. Barry Bonds has been saying all he wants to do is win a World Series ring. Well, I've played maybe a year or two less than him, and that's all that's on my mind, too."

RANDY JOHNSON CAREER STATISTICS

- Height: 6'10"
- Weight: 232 lbs.
- Throws: Left
- Bats: Right
- Born: September 10, 1963, Walnut Creek, California

SEASON	TEAM	G	GS	CG	SHO	IP	H	R	ER	HR	BB	SO	W	L	SV	HLD	BLSV	ERA
1988	MONTREAL	4	4	1	0	26.0	23	8	7	3	7	25	3	0	0	0	0	2.42
1989	SEATTLE	22	22	2	0	131.0	118	75	64	11	70	104	7	9	0	0	0	4.40
1989	MONTREAL	7	6	0	0	29.2	29	25	22	2	26	26	0	4	0	0	0	6.67
1989	TOTALS	29	28	2	0	160.2	147	100	86	13	96	130	7	13	0	0	0	4.82
1990	SEATTLE	33	33	5	2	219.2	174	103	89	26	120	194	14	11	0	0	0	3.65
1991	SEATTLE	33	33	2	1	201.1	151	96	89	15	152	228	13	10	0	0	0	3.98
1992	SEATTLE	31	31	6	2	210.1	154	104	88	13	144	241	12	14	0	0	0	3.76
1993	SEATTLE	35	34	10	3	255.1	185	97	92	22	99	308	19	8	1	0	0	3.24
1994	SEATTLE	23	23	9	4	172.0	132	65	61	14	72	204	13	6	0	0	0	3.19
1995	SEATTLE	30	30	6	3	214.1	159	65	59	12	65	294	18	2	0	0	0	2.48
1996	SEATTLE	14	8	0	0	61.1	48	27	25	8	25	85	5	0	1	0	1	3.67
1997	SEATTLE	30	29	5	2	213.0	147	60	54	20	77	291	20	4	0	0	0	2.28
1998	SEATTLE	23	23	6	2	160.0	146	90	77	19	60	213	9	10	0	0	0	4.33
1998	HOUSTON	11	11	4	4	84.1	57	12	12	4	26	116	10	1	0	0	0	1.28
1998	TOTALS	34	34	10	6	244.1	203	102	89	23	86	329	19	11	0	0	0	3.28
1999	ARIZONA	35	35	12	2	271.2	207	86	75	30	70	364	17	9	0	0	0	2.48
2000	ARIZONA	35	35	8	3	248.2	202	89	73	23	76	347	19	7	0	0	0	2.64
2001	ARIZONA	35	34	3	2	249.2	181	74	69	19	71	372	21	6	0	0	0	2.49
CAREER TOTALS		401	391	79	30	2748.1	2113	1076	956	241	1160	3412	200	101	2	0	1	3.13

"For my money, he's the most dominant pitcher of his era," Brenly said. "There might be more 20-game winners, more Cy Young Award winners, but you ask hitters who is the most dominating pitcher, the most intimidating pitcher? It's Randy Johnson."

Johnson struckout only six batters over seven innings in his next start, a 10-1 victory over the Colorado Rockies on October 2, for his 200th career win, and when the Diamondbacks clinched the Western Division title before his next start, his regular season was over. 372 strikeouts, eleven short of Ryan's Major League record and ten short of the National League record set by Sandy Koufax in 1965.

"Strikeouts are pretty irrelevant," Johnson said. "It's pretty special when you can go out and be around long enough and play on enough good teams to win 200 games. That's probably the one thing that I'm pretty proud of."

Now, all that was left was the post-season . . . and the Cy Young voting, which would take place before the playoffs started. Johnson picked up 30 out of 32 first-place votes to easily outdistance Schilling and win his fourth Cy Young. He was the second pitcher to win three consecutive Cy Young Awards. Greg Maddux of the Braves was the first.

"I'm more a pitcher than a thrower now," Johnson said. "I have a game plan now. I don't need the award to validate my commitment. I've pushed myself."

Was Johnson's 2001 season the most dominant ever by a pitcher? That's for the historians to decide. His 372 strikeouts led the league for the eighth time. He averaged a record 13.4 strikeouts per nine innings. He moved into ninth place on the all-time strikeout list, passing Hall of Famers Bob Gibson, Ferguson Jenkins and Phil Neikro. His strikeout-to-walk ratio was five-to-one. Johnson and Schilling were the first teammates to finish one-two in the Cy Young balloting since 1956.

"What helped most with Curt was that he's one of the few pitchers who knows the expectations put upon that ace in a rotation of five pitchers," Johnson said. "So I can share with him experiences and feelings I couldn't share with anybody. That's why teammates saw a side of me this year they didn't see before, like putting golf balls in the clubhouse before I pitched playoff games. I didn't have the burden I'd been carrying for years. I didn't have to come to the ballpark knowing I'd have to win this game. I felt like if we were pitching back-to-back games, if I didn't win, he would. And if he didn't, I would."

Johnson and Schilling were a one-two punch the likes of which the National League had never seen. But, even by himself, Johnson could have been described with one word: unfair.

6

ALEX RODRIGUEZ
THE 252 MILLION DOLLAR MAN STRIKES GOLD

"I wish I would have played baseball and been a shortstop."

—WAYNE GRETZKY

THERE WERE SURELY BIG WINNERS in the Las Vegas casino where Alex Rodriguez was standing in early December 2000, when his cell phone rang, but none of them had ever come close to the jackpot the 26-year-old shortstop was about to hit.

"You'd better step away from the table to a place where you can talk," agent Scott Boras told him over the phone. "I just finalized the deal with the Texas Rangers for $252-million for ten years."

"Wow, that's great!" Rodriguez exclaimed. "I can't believe it."

Nobody could. Undoubtedly, Rodriguez had the statistical numbers to warrant a big-money deal. In 2000, for the third straight season, Rodriguez finished with at least 41 homers and 111 runs batted in for the Seattle Mariners. His 132 RBIs in 2000 was the best by a shortstop in either league since 1959. Over the past three seasons, he had recorded 125 homers and 367 RBIs, almost-unheard-of numbers for a shortstop. Four appearances in the All-Star Game. An American League batting title. At age 26, fourth on the all-time list for homeruns hit as a shortstop.

But then came these numbers: 10 years, $252-million. Rodriguez's new contract with the Texas Rangers was called everything from "insane" to "catastrophic." Critics feared that the contract would result in the death of baseball. Wrote Pedro Gomez in *The Arizona Republic:* "The new class president/dunce, of course, is Texas Rangers owner Tom Hicks, who overwhelmed the sports world and Alex Rodriguez with a 10-year, $252-million contract that has set the game on its side. This quarter-billion dollar contract may very well solidify the majority of the owners to enact real change, not the cosmetic Band-Aids of recent years that have not worked. If it means shutting down the game for a full year in order to right this foundering ship, then so be it, many are hopefully thinking. Rodriguez's contract will be used repeatedly as the primary reason for the indignation of so many, maybe even some who will walk away for good if the game shuts down yet again."

Indeed, the contract did seem insane. It was twice as large as the previous record sports contract and more than what Hicks paid for the entire team and the ballpark. The franchise hadn't won a post-season series in forty years, including its eleven seasons as the Washington Senators, and was coming off a 71-91 season in which it finished last in the American League West.

On top of that, after signing A-Rod, the Rangers did nothing to improve their horrible pitching.

"People criticized me for coming to Texas and saying we don't have pitching," Rodriguez said. "I didn't sign for one year. I saw what happened in Seattle when we were close and management didn't get the big player that can put you over the top. I'm convinced Mr. Hicks will do what it takes to win. There is nothing I would like to do more than to prove him right about my contract."

Hicks stood by the signing, fending off a storm of criticism by saying, "Our judgment is that Alex will break every record in baseball before he finishes his career. He's a great asset to the community and fans. As we build this team around Alex, I think the fans in Dallas and Fort Worth will come to absolutely love him. This signing will pay huge dividends for this team and it will pay dividends for Alex and the city. He's tied to this community now. When fans realize the special personality he has to go with the special talent he has on the field, well, it's a winning combination."

And manager Johnny Oates, who would not finish the season with the Rangers, added, "If there was ever anyone worth $252 million in today's game, he's the one guy you'd probably get your money's worth out of. With our club being where we've been the last five years, I don't think making the playoffs with or without A-Rod is acceptable. This organization wants to do better than that. And I think we have a better chance with A-Rod than without him."

Nobody doubted Rodriguez's ability. People were merely questioning whether greed had reached a new high in professional sports and whether the balance of power between the have and have-not teams in baseball had reached a new high. For his part, Rodriguez refused to feel guilty about signing the richest contract in sports history.

"Somebody wins a lottery and they're a national hero," he said. "Somebody works their butt off and he's a devil. I've made the progression to this point and I can't feel guilty. It's something that doesn't concern me. I'm here to play baseball. That's what I love to do."

Rodriguez's mega-signing made an impact around the league. Chicago White Sox designated hitter Frank Thomas, who was making $9.9-million a year, looked at what A-Rod was making and decided not to show up for spring training until his contract was renegotiated. Gary Sheffield of the Dodgers decided he was being disrespected at $9-million a year and demanded a trade. Barry Bonds, a $10.3-million man, complained when the Giants didn't offer him an extension. Even smiling Sammy Sosa refused to waive his no-trade clause without a long-term extension.

"I have respect for what Gary and Barry are doing right now because they're at the top among players," said Thomas, who sud-

denly wasn't so happy with his seven-year, $66.662-million deal. "I know I'm in that category, too. You see the pay scale is getting out of whack. You can't have A-Rod making $25-million and we're coming in at seven, eight, nine million. It's like Hollywood. You can't have the top actor making $25-million and the rest making $10-million. I'm not asking to be the richest man in baseball. I just want to be in the top 20. But in the top 50? That's embarrassing."

$66.662-million? Embarrassing?

Said Bonds: "I don't want Alex Rodriguez money. I just want what I work for."

Added Sheffield: "The bottom line is all about respect."

Of course, the bottom line was, as always, about money.

The only guy who didn't seem to be complaining was the guy

who had the most right to: Rangers catcher Ivan Rodriguez, Alex's new teammate, who was making $16-million a year less than A-Rod, even though he had similar talent.

"I'm happy with my contract right now," I-Rod said. "My family was happy when I signed, so why should I be upset now?"

Ah, sanity! So unusual, it seemed insane. Of course, the plan was for Rodriguez to make his contract look like a bargain.

"If I told you that made me feel good, then every time somebody tells me I'm not worth it, it should bother me, right?" Alex told *Sports Illustrated*. "You can't have it both ways, so I don't take any of it to heart. This is the first time I've been singled out like this. It's as though I'm walking around with a sign around my neck that says 252. How will I react? I've never been in this position, so I can't tell you for sure. I think I'll be fine. I worked so hard over the winter. I turned down Leno and Letterman and lots of stuff. It's like how I approach big games or RBI situations. When the pressure's greatest, I go back to basics, to the fundamentals. I'm ready."

The Rangers were ready. "He looks great in that uniform," teammate Rafael Palmeiro said. "I can't wait until it's for real. He has stepped right in for this organization and put us on a different echelon with the great teams in baseball."

Uh, not exactly, Raffy.

So opening day arrived in San Juan, Puerto Rico, with the Rangers playing the Blue Jays, and Rodriguez cleanly handled the first ball hit to him at shortstop. Good news. Then he threw the ball wildly to first base for an error. Bad news. The next time the ball came to him, the Blue Jays had a runner at first base, but Rodriguez fell while trying to turn a doubleplay. Later in the game, he fell face-first while trying to field a grounder. A-Rod had two hits, but the Rangers lost, 8-1.

All that for $252-million, right?

"You have to start somewhere," Rodriguez said.

Not yet. In his first ten games, Rodriguez had only 11 hits, two RBIs and no homeruns. Rodriguez picked up the pace (his teammates didn't) and was hitting .362 on April 16 when he returned to play the Mariners for the first time in Seattle. The sellout crowd at

(Opposite page) The $252-million man: Alex Rodriguez tries on his new duds, a Texas Rangers jersey, during the news conference to announce his signing. Agent Scott Boras (center), who negotiated the contract, looks on while Rangers owner Tom Hicks examines his investment. The signing would outrage other teams and fans.

Safeco Field waved signs that said things like "A-WAD," "PAY-ROD," and "A-ROD PLEASE BUY ME A HOUSE." The fans threw fake money at him and booed him loudly each time he stepped to the plate. In the second game of the series, Rodriguez made two errors. He was three-for-12 in the three games and the Rangers lost twice.

By late July, the Rangers were thirty games behind the red-hot Mariners, but Rodriguez wasn't the reason. He led the Rangers in just about every offensive category—batting average, home runs, RBIs, hits, runs, doubles, total bases and slugging percentage—and was the only player on the team to play every game.

"Alex has played tremendously well," Rangers centerfielder Gabe Kapler said. "As a club, we've gotten everything we could possibly hope for out of him."

More. If it's possible for a baseball player to be worth $25-million a year, then Rodriguez was worth every penny. He set a franchise record for homeruns with 52, smashing the Major League record for shortstops. He never took a day off, starting all 162 games to become the first Ranger since 1989 to start every game in a season. He hit .318 and drove in 135 runs. And, as a mega-money guy should be, but isn't always, he was a team leader.

"Just take the last decade," wrote Evan Grant of the *Dallas Morning News*. "Nolan Ryan was hardly around when he wasn't pitching. Will Clark's volume was much more noticeable than the substance of his message. Rodriguez's leadership extends well beyond being the face of the club and handing out a few trinkets. He has been instrumental in getting teammates to communicate . . . He has taken to meeting regularly with the day's starting pitcher. Since spring training, he has reached out to the future of the Rangers' infield, striking up strong relationships with Michael Young and Carlos Pena. At ease in both English and Spanish, he has been able to bridge and break down many of the clubhouse cliques that existed in recent seasons."

Said interim manager Jerry Narron: "From what I've seen, he's an incredibly talented player and an even better man."

A-Rod more than helped the Rangers get their money back. Merchandise with his name on it outsold all other merchandise at

ALEX RODRIGUEZ CAREER STATISTICS

- Height: 6'3"
- Weight: 215 lbs.
- Throws: Right
- Bats: Right
- Born: July 27, 1975, New York, New York

SEASON	TEAM	G	AB	R	H	2B	3B	HR	RBI	BB	SO	SB	CS	OBP	SLG	OPS	AVG
1994	SEATTLE	17	54	4	11	0	0	0	2	3	20	3	0	.241	.204	.445	.204
1995	SEATTLE	48	142	15	33	6	2	5	19	6	42	4	2	.264	.408	.672	.232
1996	SEATTLE	146	601	141	215	54	1	36	123	59	104	15	4	.414	.631	1.045	.358
1997	SEATTLE	141	587	100	176	40	3	23	84	41	99	29	6	.350	.496	.846	.300
1998	SEATTLE	161	686	123	213	35	5	42	124	45	121	46	13	.360	.560	.920	.310
1999	SEATTLE	129	502	110	143	25	0	42	111	56	109	21	7	.357	.586	.943	.285
2000	SEATTLE	148	554	134	175	34	2	41	132	100	121	15	4	.420	.606	1.026	.316
2001	TEXAS	162	632	133	201	34	1	52	135	75	131	18	3	.399	.622	1.021	.318
CAREER TOTALS		952	3758	760	1167	228	14	241	730	385	747	151	39	.378	.571	.949	.311

The Ballpark in Arlington, eclipsing even Ivan Rodriguez, who had been the most popular Ranger.

Rodriguez was truly marvelous, even when his teammates were horrible. In mid-May, he had eight hits in three games. The Rangers lost two of those games. He had four three-hit games in July alone and a four-hit game in August in a 19-6 loss to the Tigers. Perhaps the Rangers' biggest mistake was spending too much on Rodriguez and not enough on acquiring other players.

The 2001 season was, arguably, Rodriguez's best season ever. In the third inning on September 23 at The Ballpark, he hit his 48th homer of the season, breaking Ernie Banks's record for homeruns by a shortstop in one season. The record had stood since 1958. Said Banks in a written statement, "Congratulations, A-Rod. I knew you could do it. You are a great man, an impressive ball player and a role model. I love the game of baseball, and I love to see players with heart and drive like yours who continue the spirit of the game."

Said Rodriguez: "This was a fun ride, but I've still got a long way to go to catch up with Ernie Banks for his career."

The ride continued. Three days later, Rodriguez was breaking more records. He hit his 49th homer of the season against the Mariners to set a Major League record for homers by an infielder other than a first baseman and break the 32-year-old franchise record for homers, previously held by Frank Howard.

The Rangers finished last again, 43 games behind the Mariners, but by season's end, nobody was calling A-Rod greedy anymore.

7

RICKEY HENDERSON
BREAKS RUTH'S WALKS RECORD, COBB'S RUNS RECORD, AND GETS HIS 3,000TH CAREER HIT

RICKEY HENDERSON WILL NEVER BE a fan favorite. Although he is undoubtedly one of the greatest players of all-time and, according to Seattle Mariners manager Lou Piniella, a surefire first-ballot Hall of Famer, he has always been viewed as a selfish, egotistical, me-first player, the type of guy who would sit in the clubhouse playing cards while his team was playing its most important game of the year.

But in a record-breaking season during which Cal Ripken Jr. and Tony Gwynn were saying their farewells to baseball, the Seattle Mariners were piling up victories, Barry Bonds was hitting one homerun after another, and the Arizona Diamondbacks were becoming the youngest expansion team to win the World Series, Henderson not only broke more records than anyone else, but he actually got some respect from the rest of baseball.

"He's been amazing," Philadelphia Phillies manager Larry Bowa

Rickey Henderson connects for a solo homerun in the third inning against the Los Angeles Dodgers on October 4, 2001, to score his 2,246th career run, passing Ty Cobb on the all-time runs list.

said. "He's been the leadoff hitter that everybody tries to get. It seems like they're diminishing more and more. You don't have that type of hitter who likes to hit oh-two all the time, who's willing to take a lot of pitches. It's something he takes a lot of pride in. With pitchers, he disrupts their rhythm. The game has evolved into homeruns. As a manager right now, I would much rather have him. A guy like Rickey disrupts your infielders, your pitchers, your outfielders. He disrupts everybody. Hitting goes in slumps, but speed never goes in slumps."

Henderson has seemingly never been mired in long slumps, and the marks he set in 2001 are testament to his longevity and consistency. At age 42, the man who long ago set the Major League record for career stolen bases, did this:

- Drew his 2,063rd base on balls, moving him past Babe Ruth and into first place on the all-time walks list.
- Scored his 2,246th run to break Ty Cobb's all-time mark for runs scored.
- Became the 25th player in Major League history to record his 3,000th career hit.

And said all the right things.

"This is the one," Henderson said as he approached the runs record. "This means more than any other record, 'cause this is really a team record. I got to rely on my teammates to go out and drive me in."

Who woulda thunk it? Rickey Henderson giving credit to his teammates? Rickey Henderson not talking about himself in the third person? Rickey Henderson . . . likeable?

"Rickey has had just a fabulous career," Piniella said. "He has been the prototype leadoff guy for I don't know how many years now. He has the rare speed and power combination. He has just had a Hall of Fame career. He competes well. Look at what he's done. His record speaks for itself. He has been just a great player his entire career. He's a first-ballot Hall of Famer."

If there were any doubts, he erased them in 2001. When spring training started, Henderson was doubtful to even get the chance to break the records. His career appeared to be over until he signed a minor league contract with the San Diego Padres in late March after every other club in the Majors had passed on his services. He started the season at Triple-A Portland before the Padres called him up on April 17. Then he went on his record-breaking run.

Milestone One: April 25 in San Diego. Henderson walked on a 3-1 pitch from Philadelphia reliever Jose Mesa leading off the ninth inning to break Ruth's record. After ball four, he tossed his bat aside, jogged to first base, shook hands with first-base coach Alan Trammell, tipped his batting helmet and acknowledged a standing ovation from the Qualcomm Stadium crowd of 12,573 by blowing kisses.

"The record is outstanding," Henderson said afterwards. "It's

(Opposite page) Rickey Henderson holds up a gold-plated commemorative home plate presented to him after he scored his 2,246th career run. A few days after the season ended, Henderson would dig the real plate out of the ground at Qualcomm Stadium in San Diego.

great to be in a class with Babe Ruth. I feel great about breaking this record by one of the greatest ballplayers who ever played this game. He was Mr. Baseball. He was the one who gave me the motivation to go out and play baseball and make this game a fun game. It seems like he had a lot of fun."

Said Phillies first baseman Travis Lee, who stood a few feet away as Henderson touched first: "That was awesome. If you think about it, that's twenty years of 100-plus walks a year. Not many guys are going to play this game for that long."

As the Padres' difficult season wore on, Tony Gwynn's occasional at-bats in his final season and Henderson's run at two more marks—the runs record and the 3,000-hit club—became the only reasons to attend games at Qualcomm Stadium. Henderson was hot early and helped the Padres climb into first place for a few days, cooled off, and by the end of the season was sharing playing time, yet he kept the records plainly in sight . . . especially Cobb's record.

"Maybe I'll get the chance to dust myself off," he said of his plans to slide across home plate with the record-breaking run. "When I was a kid, I always felt when I had to come home, I had to be dirty or my mom would always say, 'You were not playing baseball.' I was always diving in the dirt trying to score runs, so I guess that's the way to go."

Milestone Two: Henderson tied Cobb's record on October 3 at Qualcomm Stadium when he scored in the third inning on a two-run double by Ryan Klesko.

"When he hit the ball down the line, I felt I had a good chance," Henderson said. "I got excited when I crossed the plate."

He broke Cobb's mark in style the next afternoon, October 4, also against Los Angeles. Leading off the third inning, Henderson hit a one-oh pitch by Dodgers righty Luke Prokopec over the leftfield fence. He raced around the bases at full speed, clapping his hands and pumping his arms, and—as promised—slid into home plate with his 2,246th run. When he got up, he was mobbed by his teammates. Gwynn emerged from the dugout smiling and carrying a gold-plated replica of home plate inscribed with a message honor-

ing Henderson. Rickey picked up the plate, raised it above his head and took in the fans' cheers.

"The slide into home plate was really a treat for my teammates," Henderson said. "They were expecting me to go head first into home plate, but I told them I hate sliding into home plate head first, so I slid in feet first. It was a thrill for them. I guess it made their day as well as mine."

Said Gwynn: "Rickey was happy and relieved. He was happy to have it over with, at least that part of it. I told him that our fans have never seen a thing like that. We may have had Lou Brock's 3,000th hit against the Padres, but as far as I know, none of that's ever happened in San Diego. And our fans, they want to be a part of that. They want to see that."

The record was played for all the drama it was worth. The homerun was replayed over and over on the Jumbotron scoreboard. In the fifth inning, Henderson was introduced as "baseball's all-time runs-scoring leader." Henderson scored his 2,246th run in his 2,976th game. Cobb had 2,245 runs in 3,035 games.

"I'm very honored, and it's a privilege to play with Rickey," teammate Mark Kotsay said. " It's an amazing feat, and when he did it, I was sitting on the bench figuring out that it's 100 runs a year. I was thinking, what's his highest run total of the year? And I checked: 148 and 137 the next year. It's a team record in a sense, but he had a lot to do with it because he's stealing bases, he's drawing walks and he's playing the game the way it's supposed to be played."

Milestone Three: Henderson waited until October 7, the final day of the season and Gwynn's retirement game, to become the 25th member of the 3,000-hit club. He had originally planned to take the day off out of deference to Gwynn, who eventually talked him into playing. In the bottom of the first inning, Henderson swung at the first pitch by Colorado's John Thompson and looped it down the rightfield line for a double. As he rounded first base, Henderson stopped, watched the ball land five feet inside the line and sprinted for second.

"I wanted to stop and run out and get the ball," Henderson said. "Then I decided to run for second. It was a miracle to me. As I'm

RICKEY HENDERSON CAREER STATISTICS

- Height: 5'10"
- Weight: 190 lbs.
- Throws: Left
- Bats: Right
- Born: December 25, 1958, Chicago, Illinois

SEASON	TEAM	G	AB	R	H	2B	3B	HR	RBI	BB	SO	SB	CS	OBP	SLG	OPS	AVG
1979	OAKLAND	89	351	49	96	13	3	1	26	34	39	33	11	.338	.336	.674	.274
1980	OAKLAND	158	591	111	179	22	4	9	53	117	54	100	26	.420	.399	.819	.303
1981	OAKLAND	108	423	89	135	18	7	6	35	64	68	56	22	.408	.437	.845	.319
1982	OAKLAND	149	536	119	143	24	4	10	51	116	94	130	42	.398	.382	.780	.267
1983	OAKLAND	145	513	105	150	25	7	9	48	103	80	108	19	.414	.421	.835	.292
1984	OAKLAND	142	502	113	147	27	4	16	58	86	81	66	18	.399	.458	.857	.293
1985	YANKEES	143	547	146	172	28	5	24	72	99	65	80	10	.419	.516	.935	.314
1986	YANKEES	153	608	130	160	31	5	28	74	89	81	87	18	.358	.469	.827	.263
1987	YANKEES	95	358	78	104	17	3	17	37	80	52	41	8	.423	.497	.920	.291
1988	YANKEES	140	554	118	169	30	2	6	50	82	54	93	13	.394	.399	.793	.305
1989	YANKEES	65	235	41	58	13	1	3	22	56	29	25	8	.392	.349	.741	.247
1989	OAKLAND	85	306	72	90	13	2	9	35	70	39	52	6	.425	.438	.863	.294
1989	TOTALS	150	541	113	148	26	3	12	57	126	68	77	14	.411	.399	.810	.274
1990	OAKLAND	136	489	119	159	33	3	28	61	97	60	65	10	.439	.577	1.016	.325
1991	OAKLAND	134	470	105	126	17	1	18	57	98	73	58	18	.400	.423	.823	.268
1992	OAKLAND	117	396	77	112	18	3	15	46	95	56	48	11	.426	.457	.883	.283
1993	OAKLAND	90	318	77	104	19	1	17	47	85	46	31	6	.469	.553	1.022	.327
1993	TORONTOONTO	44	163	37	35	3	1	4	12	35	19	22	2	.356	.319	.675	.215
1993	TOTALS	134	481	114	139	22	2	21	59	120	65	53	8	.432	.474	.906	.289
1994	OAKLAND	87	296	66	77	13	0	6	20	72	45	22	7	.411	.365	.776	.260
1995	OAKLAND	112	407	67	122	31	1	9	54	72	66	32	10	.407	.447	.854	.300
1996	SAN DIEGO	148	465	110	112	17	2	9	29	125	90	37	15	.410	.344	.754	.241
1997	ANAHEIM	32	115	21	21	3	0	2	7	26	23	16	4	.343	.261	.604	.183
1997	SAN DIEGO	88	288	63	79	11	0	6	27	71	62	29	4	.422	.375	.797	.274
1997	TOTALS	120	403	84	100	14	0	8	34	97	85	45	8	.400	.342	.742	.248
1998	OAKLAND	152	542	101	128	16	1	14	57	118	114	66	13	.376	.347	.723	.236
1999	METS	121	438	89	138	30	0	12	42	82	82	37	14	.423	.466	.889	.315
2000	SEATTLE	92	324	58	77	13	2	4	30	63	55	31	9	.362	.327	.689	.238
2000	METS	31	96	17	21	1	0	0	2	25	20	5	2	.387	.229	.616	.219
2000	TOTALS	123	420	75	98	14	2	4	32	88	75	36	11	.368	.305	.673	.233
2001	SAN DIEGO	123	379	70	86	17	3	8	42	81	84	25	7	.366	.351	.717	.227
CAREER TOTALS		2979	10710	2248	3000	503	65	290	1094	2141	1631	1395	333	.402	.420	.822	.280

running, I'm remembering that the hit I got for 3,000 is the exact hit I got for my first hit. It's a great feeling, a feeling that you can't really describe. It was sweet especially on Tony Gwynn's day. See us old guys, we've still got a little something."

Said Gwynn: "Man, what a sight, Rickey cruising into second base and all his teammates running out there. That's what the game's all about. He's the all-time leader in steals, walks and runs scored, and today, he steps up to the plate and gets it done. Of all the things I wanted to have happen today, Rickey getting his 3,000th hit was at the top of the list."

Gwynn and Henderson were the only teammates in National League history to have at least 3,000 hits each.

A few days later, with the season over and the stadium empty, Henderson used a sledgehammer to remove homeplate from the ground. The plate had been anchored into an aluminum stand with concrete and spikes. Henderson used twenty whacks to get it out.

"He walked out arm-in-arm with the baby," said stadium manager Bill Wilson.

This one was totally for Rickey.

TONY GWYNN
GOODBYE, MR. GWYNN

"Just throw it down the middle. Then hope he hits it at somebody."

— MIKE PIAZZA

"He can hit anything and anybody. Doesn't matter who's throwing. Lefty, righty, octopi."

— MARK GRACE

There will never be a Legend of Tony Gwynn. Fifty years from now, grandfathers won't sit around telling their grandchildren about the time Gwynn hit three homers in one World Series game (because he didn't), or about the time he used his superhuman strength to bully a high inside curve ball over the rightfield fence to win a game (he didn't do that, either). He never hit more than 17 homers in a season. He never had more than 119 RBIs. He never won a World Series. And he played his entire career in San

(Opposite page) Tony Gwynn got his final hit, a double, in the sixth inning of the Padres' game against the Colorado Rockies on October 7, then acknowledged the crowd's cheers. He played his final game the next day.

Diego, a city overshadowed not only by Los Angeles a few hours to the north, but by just about every sports city in America.

Tony Gwynn wasn't a superhero. He wasn't The Iron Man, like Cal Ripken. Chances are that if Gwynn and Ripken walked down the street of any city in the United States except San Diego, kids would go running up to Ripken, asking for his autograph and, "by the way, who's your friend?"

Ripken got most of the attention and the endorsements. But if you're going to compare careers, then Gwynn was head and shoulders above Ripken, whose career was defined by one number: 2,131 consecutive games played. The numbers are all on Gwynn's side.

Career batting average: .338, the 17th best ever.

National League batting titles: Eight, including four in a row, joining Hall of Famer Honus Wagner as the only two players to do so.

During seasons in which he had enough at-bats to qualify for the batting title, he never failed to finish in the top eight in batting average. He batted less than .300 only once in 20 Major League seasons, and that was in his first season, 1982.

And Gwynn was one of only four National League players to play 20 seasons and his entire career with one team.

Three future Hall of Famers, Gwynn, Mark McGwire, and Ripken, retired in 2001, and while Ripken got all the attention, Gwynn—quiet as a man, quiet as a player—was the greatest one to retire.

"If people talk about the toughest hitters I've ever had to face, he is definitely at the top of the list," pitcher David Cone said. "A great professional and a great hitter, and a one-town guy, too. He's a rare combination."

After battling serious knee and hamstring problems for two seasons, Gwynn announced his retirement on June 28, 2001, in San Diego. But even with bad knees, the man who studied hitting like few others became a premier pinch-hitter in his final season and walked out of the game a .324 hitter.

"I love what I do," Gwynn said. "Whether you're doing it four times a game or one time, you're still getting a chance to do it. I can't

do things the way I always did. I'm not going to go out to rightfield and jeopardize my team's chances of winning because I want to be in the lineup. In the National League, you don't have the luxury of being the designated hitter. You have to learn to be honest."

He was always an honest player, even if he paid far more attention to his swing than he did to his girth. Former big-leaguer John Kruk, who played rookie ball with Gwynn, once said, "Where I was raised, if you wanted to be successful, you found somebody successful and followed their lead. I followed Tony Gwynn from the start. I followed him to McDonald's. I followed him to Burger King."

But Kruk played only ten seasons, Gwynn played twenty, and it's unlikely baseball will see another one like him for a long time. In an era of homerun-crazy big swingers, Gwynn was a contact hitter whose main goal was reaching first base. He was a perfectionist who couldn't deal with the main fact of life in baseball, that even the best hitters are successful only a third of the time. He'd bring a VCR with him on the road so he could watch replays of his at-bats in his hotel room. At home, he spent more time than anybody else in the batting cage. Gwynn was a student of hitting science who actually became a better hitter in the second half of his career than he was in the first half. His best season was in 1994, when he hit .394.

"For me, it's easier to see the greatness in other players than it is to see it in myself," Gwynn said. "I just play. I love to play and I go out and try to play the best I can. And where people rate you or what category they put you in, that's for other people to do. I was happy that I was pretty consistent, pretty much went about my business the same way every day. I'm happy that I played 20 years, and I've played them all here in San Diego, and so the back of my bubble gum card from here to eternity will look pretty good.

"Winning my first Gold Glove [in 1986] is still one of the highlights of my career. When I came into this game, I was a guy who could just swing the bat. I had to work really hard at the other facets of the game. And I never got great at it, but I felt like I was getting to the point where I was pretty good. Getting 3,000 hits was special, too. But I'm happier about the fact that I've been able to play longer than just about anything else. Coming up, I didn't know what to expect. I didn't know what kind of player I would be."

Perhaps even Gwynn didn't realize how much he was appreciated until his farewell tour. He went from city-to-city and was feted in each place.

"Sometimes when you play down here, you don't know if people are watching, so it has been beautiful to see Tony being honored as we go to these cities for the last time," said Padres third base coach Tim Flannery during Gwynn's farewell tour. "It makes us all stop and consider what Tony has done. Not just the statistics, but what it takes to live this lifestyle for twenty years, the travel and having to be Tony Gwynn. Wherever you go, people know you and want a little piece of you."

As his final season wound down, and he spent more time on the bench, Gwynn announced that he wouldn't be leaving baseball entirely. In fact, he'd be as much a part of it as ever as the head baseball coach at San Diego State, his alma mater. Days before his last game at Qualcomm Stadium in San Diego, Gwynn reflected on his career.

"I'm about to put on a big league uniform for the last time ever, and it might surprise some people to know that I'm very happy about it," Gwynn told MLB.com. "It will be emotional when it's all over, but I'm a very happy man.

"For me, the homerun in the World Series in '98 was probably my biggest personal moment, the one big hit for me," Gwynn said. "Not necessarily because it was a home run, but because for years, people said I was afraid to play in the big game. You know, play on the big stage. And as far as I'm concerned, that hit shoved it right in their faces. I played in the World Series where we got beat four games to none, but I hit .500. You can look at the numbers and say I had a good series, but to me what stands out is I had four hits at home and four hits on the road. I went four-for-eight in New York and four-for-eight here in San Diego. And that's my career. I've been consistent year in and year out. That's what you try to do.

"You can look at the eight batting titles, the All-Star Games, the Gold Gloves, hitting .300 all those times, all the things that look really good on the resume, but the bottom line for me was, 'How was he over 162?' And over 162, I don't think anyone's been close to doing what I've done. That's why I say I feel good about it. I'm not going to sit here and apologize for it. That's the type of player I was, and that's what I did.

"People ask me all the time where I think I fit in with guys like Mr. Williams and all those other guys. I don't look at myself in that light because it's not for me to say. It's for the fans, it's for people who've watched me play to put me where they think I should go. And that's the beauty of the game. There will be arguments from now until the day I die about where I fit in the big picture and as far as I'm concerned, when I'm through, I'm through. I don't have to talk about it anymore. I don't have to do anything about it. People can categorize me however they want to. They can slice and dice the numbers however they want to. But for me, it's just about, 'Did I do it the right way?' That's the only question I have. I think most people will tell you they think I did it the right way and that's all that matters to me.

"For other people, it's going to be different coming to Padres games because I'm not going to be here. For them, when they come and watch a Padres game, they're used to seeing No. 19 somewhere. And they're not going to see No. 19 anymore. It gets back to what I said ten years ago. At some point, people are going to realize they had a good thing and it's not going to be here anymore. For us contact hitters, that was our creed: you just keep doing it, day in and day out and eventually someone will notice. Well, we're getting to the end now and people have noticed, and the reaction that I'm getting this year tells me I did it the right way."

Gwynn's sendoff on October 7, 2001, in San Diego was far more restrained than Ripken's in Baltimore. He didn't play until the ninth inning, when he pinch-hit with one out. Gwynn received a standing ovation from the crowd of 60,103 as he made his way to the plate, waved his batting helmet several times and grounded out to shortstop in his 9,288th and final at-bat.

After the game, Gwynn was honored in a ceremony. Sportscaster Bob Costas narrated highlights of his career. Players from the 1982

TONY GWYNN CAREER STATISTICS

- Height: 5'11"
- Weight: 225 lbs.
- Throws: Left
- Bats: Left
- Born: May 9, 1960, Los Angeles, California

SEASON	TEAM	G	AB	R	H	2B	3B	HR	RBI	BB	SO	SB	CS	OBP	SLG	OPS	AVG
1982	SAN DIEGO	54	190	33	55	12	2	1	17	14	16	8	3	.337	.389	.726	.289
1983	SAN DIEGO	86	304	34	94	12	2	1	37	23	21	7	4	.355	.372	.727	.309
1984	SAN DIEGO	158	606	88	213	21	10	5	71	59	23	33	18	.410	.444	.854	.351
1985	SAN DIEGO	154	622	90	197	29	5	6	46	45	33	14	11	.364	.408	.772	.317
1986	SAN DIEGO	160	642	107	211	33	7	14	59	52	35	37	9	.381	.467	.848	.329
1987	SAN DIEGO	157	589	119	218	36	13	7	54	82	35	56	12	.447	.511	.958	.370
1988	SAN DIEGO	133	521	64	163	22	5	7	70	51	40	26	11	.373	.415	.788	.313
1989	SAN DIEGO	158	604	82	203	27	7	4	62	56	30	40	16	.389	.424	.813	.336
1990	SAN DIEGO	141	573	79	177	29	10	4	72	44	23	17	8	.357	.415	.772	.309
1991	SAN DIEGO	134	530	69	168	27	11	4	62	34	19	8	8	.355	.432	.787	.317
1992	SAN DIEGO	128	520	77	165	27	3	6	41	46	16	3	6	.371	.415	.786	.317
1993	SAN DIEGO	122	489	70	175	41	3	7	59	36	19	14	1	.398	.497	.895	.358
1994	SAN DIEGO	110	419	79	165	35	1	12	64	48	19	5	0	.454	.568	1.022	.394
1995	SAN DIEGO	135	535	82	197	33	1	9	90	35	15	17	5	.404	.484	.888	.368
1996	SAN DIEGO	116	451	67	159	27	2	3	50	39	17	11	4	.400	.441	.841	.353
1997	SAN DIEGO	149	592	97	220	49	2	17	119	43	28	12	5	.409	.547	.956	.372
1998	SAN DIEGO	127	461	65	148	35	0	16	69	35	18	3	1	.364	.501	.865	.321
1999	SAN DIEGO	111	411	59	139	27	0	10	62	29	14	7	2	.381	.477	.858	.338
2000	SAN DIEGO	36	127	17	41	12	0	1	17	9	4	0	1	.364	.441	.805	.323
2001	SAN DIEGO	71	102	5	33	9	1	1	17	10	9	1	0	.384	.461	.845	.324
CAREER TOTALS		2440	9288	1383	3141	543	85	135	1138	790	434	319	125	.388	.459	.847	.338

Padres, Gwynn's first team, made a surprise appearance. Gwynn's current teammates gave him a Harley Davidson motorcycle. The Padres announced that he had been unanimously elected to the team's Hall of Fame and that the team's new stadium would be located at 19 Tony Gwynn Drive.

Then Gwynn took the microphone, again acknowledged the crowd's cheers and said, "I would like people to say that I played the game the way it was supposed to be played."

There's no doubt that he did.

CAL RIPKEN, JR.
THE IRON MAN CALLS IT QUITS

THE NEWS CONFERENCE WAS SCHEDULED for three P.M. on June 19, 2001. Cal Ripken, Jr., and his wife, Kelly, showed up fashionably late. They walked into the party room on the sixth floor of the B&O Warehouse outside Camden Yards at 3:36, as if the decision that many had long considered inevitable had been delayed again. But for Ripken, who would turn 40 in two months, nothing was inevitable: not the end of his Iron Man streak for consecutive games played, which ended in 1998, and not the end of his playing career. He had been tormented by the decision.

Finally, however, Ripken stepped to the podium. He was wearing slacks and a sports shirt, and he didn't look tormented at all. He looked relieved when he announced that he would retire at the end of the season.

"I didn't feel any pressure up to this point or any other point to make a decision," said Ripken, who played for only one team, the Baltimore Orioles, in his career. "It's totally a personal decision. It came from within me. And I paid attention to the signs that were pulling at me. There was no push. There was a pull that helped me make the decision."

Orioles owner Peter Angelos didn't attend the news conference, but he issued a statement that echoed the feelings of all baseball fans: "Cal's remarkable record-setting statistics as a player are only part of his astonishing story. His work ethic, his constant striving for excellence and his many contributions back to his community have established him as a role model for players and fans alike. Cal Ripken has shown he loves the game of baseball, but I speak for many when I say that baseball loves him as well."

Long after Ripken had broken Lou Gehrig's Iron Man streak and his consecutive games played streak had reached into the upper two thousands, many critics suggested that Ripken didn't know when to sit down. But this time, he clearly knew the time had come. When he announced his retirement, Ripken was hitting .207 with only four homeruns and 25 RBIs. Several young Orioles needed his playing time in order to develop, but Ripken insisted his lagging production had nothing to do with his decision.

"Could I stick my chest out a little further and be happier and less frustrated from a baseball perspective?" Ripken said. "Absolutely. But ultimately it wouldn't change my feelings for the other projects and the challenges that are ahead of me outside my playing career. It wouldn't change my feeling the need to be closer to my family. To fully understand that is to understand the lifestyle I've led my whole life."

Said Orioles manager Mike Hargrove: "I don't think there was any doubt that Cal was going to make this decision for himself. I don't think there was anything that we could do or wanted to do to force Cal to make this decision. People earn things, and Cal has certainly earned the right to say when he wants to go."

He was, in addition to his records, an unusual player. Ripken was an Oriole from the time the organization selected him in the second round of the free-agent draft on June 6, 1978. The first time he was on the disabled list was April 18, 1999. He never demanded a trade, even when the Orioles were a struggling team. He never tested the free-agent market, even when he could have named his price. He carried himself like a working class man, showing up to work every day, and although he wasn't a natural hitter, he compensated with strength, intelligence and hard work and retired as the Orioles' all-time leader in hits (3,184), runs (1,647), doubles (603), homeruns (431) and RBIs (1,695). Of course, his most significant number is 2,632, the consecutive games he played.

"When I look back over my career, I tried to maximize my playing opportunity and tried to love every moment I had on the field," Ripken said. "So when I look back, I don't have those kind of regrets. I accomplished what my skills, my ability and my determination allowed me to, and I'm proud of the experience."

For many baseball fans, the lasting image of Ripken will be his performance in the 2001 All-Star Game, his last. It was like something out of a fable: the retiring hero stepping to the plate in front of an international audience and doing exactly what everyone expected him to do.

The game was played at Safeco Field in Seattle on July 10. A sellout crowd of 47,364. Perfect weather. The Mid-Summer Classic. The National League and the American League were scoreless in the bottom of the third inning when Ripken came to bat.

The evening had already been emotional for Ripken. He had been chosen to the AL squad despite unimpressive batting statistics in the first half of the season: .240 batting average with four homers and 28 RBIs. He jogged out to play third base in the top of the first inning, but was cut off by Alex Rodriguez, the superstar shortstop who had been inspired by Ripken to play that position. Rodriguez ran toward third base and nudged Ripken toward shortstop, a position he hadn't played since mid-1997. Ripken hesitated.

"I must have been the only person on the whole planet who didn't know," he said. "I went out there and thought this wasn't the time or the place to go back to short."

"Everybody's expecting you to do it," Rodriguez said. "Go on over there."

It was a public display of respect and affection for Ripken, and both the crowd and the man appreciated the gesture. Rodriguez moved to shortstop and Ripken went back to third for the top of the second inning.

"It was a really neat tribute," Ripken said. "I spent most of my

career at shortstop. It was great being at shortstop again. I appreciated it."

Los Angeles Dodgers pitcher Chan Ho Park replaced Randy Johnson for the National League in the bottom of the third inning. Ripken stepped to the plate to lead off, and the crowd stood and cheered. Ripken stepped from the batter's box, tipped his helmet to the fans and waved his bat.

"Coming to the plate, I was excited," Ripken said. "I was a little worried about the shadows. I was in the cage swinging hard trying to get ready. I went up there thinking, Gosh, it's hard to see. Let's keep things short and put things in play. I tried to acknowledge the fans very quickly because I didn't want the game to be delayed for that."

Park wound up and threw a fastball down the middle of the plate—a batting practice pitch that hung forever. Ripken took one step and swung. He made solid contact and lined the ball toward the bullpen in leftfield. For a moment, time slowed. Ripken looked up with the crowd as he ran towards first base. There was never any doubt. The ball landed 392 feet away in the leftfield bullpen for Ripken's second All-Star Game homer. At 40 years, 10 months and 10 days, he had become the oldest man to homer in an All-Star Game, beating Stan "The Man" Musial by over a year.

"I swung and made good contact," Ripken said. "The ball went out of the ballpark. And I felt like I was flying around the bases."

"It was really magical," American League manager Joe Torre said. "Cal is such a class individual, and his legacy in baseball is not just going to be how he played, but the way he played, the way he carried himself. It was wonderful."

After touching home plate, with the crowd roaring louder than before and with players on both sides still cheering, Ripken slapped hands with Torre and couldn't control a beaming smile. Out on the field, Texas Rangers catcher Ivan Rodriguez stepped into the batter's box. The fans, who had settled down momentarily, got up again and cheered. Rodriguez stepped out of the batter's box and Ripken moved up the dugout steps and waved his helmet.

"It was like a dream come true," Sammy Sosa said. "Everybody

(Opposite page) The Iron Man's final ride: Cal Ripken Jr. enjoys the cheers of the crowd at Camden Yards in Baltimore after playing his final game on October 6, 2001.

was on their feet and clapping, and, after that, he came in with the homerun. That's amazing. He is The Man."

Said Kirby Puckett, "I couldn't believe it. It was unreal. The rest of us sit and dream. Cal dreams, and then he does it."

The evening was like a theatrical event. After grounding out in his second at-bat in the bottom of the fifth, Ripken walked out to third base to start the sixth inning. The AL players warmed up as video highlights of Ripken and Tony Gwynn played on the Safeco Field scoreboard. As if on cue, Troy Glaus of the Anaheim Angels jogged to third base to relieve Ripken. Ripken walked away, Gwynn walked onto the field, and the evening's second-most memorable event began. Players from both teams ran out of both dugouts to show their appreciation for two of the greatest players of the past twenty years. During a rare mid-game ceremony that lasted six minutes, Ripken and Tony Gwynn received the Commissioner's Historic Achievement Award.

The American League went on to win the game, 4-1, and Ripken earned his second All-Star Game MVP.

"I think we appreciate everything a whole lot more at the end," Ripken said afterward. "It's been a whirlwind, a great atmosphere, a great climate. I always thought the All-Star Game was a special time to celebrate baseball. It meant something special for our family to sit around and watch it on TV. This one I came into with my eyes wider looking to take advantage of everything."

He even watched the final three innings of the game on the bench with his son, Ryan. Ripken's final All-Star Game numbers: 19 appearances, including 14 at shortstop, breaking Ozzie Smith's record.

The rest of the season turned into the Cal Ripken Farewell Tour that he had insisted he didn't want. In Miami, the Marlins honored Ripken with a ceremony that included former Orioles manager Earl Weaver, and the fans honored him with a standing ovation before each at-bat. In Texas, the Rangers retired Ripken's locker in the visitor's clubhouse, and Hall of Fame pitcher Nolan Ryan was on hand to present Ripken with cowboy boots, a signed Rangers jersey and a $15,000 donation to charity. In Anaheim, Ripken and his family

CAL RIPKEN JR. CAREER STATISTICS

- Height: 6'4"
- Weight: 220 lbs.
- Throws: Right
- Bats: Right
- Born: August 24, 1960, Havre de Grace, Maryland

SEASON	TEAM	G	AB	R	H	2B	3B	HR	RBI	BB	SO	SB	CS	OBP	SLG	OPS	AVG
1981	BALTIMORE	23	39	1	5	0	0	0	0	1	8	0	0	.150	.128	.278	.128
1982	BALTIMORE	160	598	90	158	32	5	28	93	46	95	3	3	.317	.475	.792	.264
1983	BALTIMORE	162	663	121	211	47	2	27	102	58	97	0	4	.371	.517	.888	.318
1984	BALTIMORE	162	641	103	195	37	7	27	86	71	89	2	1	.374	.510	.884	.304
1985	BALTIMORE	161	642	116	181	32	5	26	110	67	68	2	3	.347	.469	.816	.282
1986	BALTIMORE	162	627	98	177	35	1	25	81	70	60	4	2	.355	.461	.816	.282
1987	BALTIMORE	162	624	97	157	28	3	27	98	81	77	3	5	.333	.436	.769	.252
1988	BALTIMORE	161	575	87	152	25	1	23	81	102	69	2	2	.372	.431	.803	.264
1989	BALTIMORE	162	646	80	166	30	0	21	93	57	72	3	2	.317	.401	.718	.257
1990	BALTIMORE	161	600	78	150	28	4	21	84	82	66	3	1	.341	.415	.756	.250
1991	BALTIMORE	162	650	99	210	46	5	34	114	53	46	6	1	.374	.566	.940	.323
1992	BALTIMORE	162	637	73	160	29	1	14	72	64	50	4	3	.323	.366	.689	.251
1993	BALTIMORE	162	641	87	165	26	3	24	90	65	58	1	4	.329	.420	.749	.257
1994	BALTIMORE	112	444	71	140	19	3	13	75	32	41	1	0	.364	.459	.823	.315
1995	BALTIMORE	144	550	71	144	33	2	17	88	52	59	0	1	.324	.422	.746	.262
1996	BALTIMORE	163	640	94	178	40	1	26	102	59	78	1	2	.341	.466	.807	.278
1997	BALTIMORE	162	615	79	166	30	0	17	84	56	73	1	0	.331	.402	.733	.270
1998	BALTIMORE	161	601	65	163	27	1	14	61	51	68	0	2	.331	.389	.720	.271
1999	BALTIMORE	86	332	51	113	27	0	18	57	13	31	0	1	.368	.584	.952	.340
2000	BALTIMORE	83	309	43	79	16	0	15	56	23	37	0	0	.310	.453	.763	.256
2001	BALTIMORE	128	477	43	114	16	0	14	68	26	63	0	2	.276	.361	.637	.239
CAREER TOTALS		3001	11551	1647	3184	603	44	431	1695	1129	1305	36	39	.340	.447	.787	.276

took part in a parade at Disneyland. In Oakland, the A's had a three-day Celebration of Cal, and the City of Oakland dedicated an inner-city baseball field in Ripken's name. In Seattle, Mariners players came out one-by-one to shake his hand, and a plaque in his honor was hung in the visitor's bullpen near where his All-Star Game homer landed. The Red Sox gave Ripken an actual box seat.

And at Yankee Stadium, the place where the original Iron Man, Lou Gehrig, played and gave his famous retirement speech—"I am the luckiest man on the face of the Earth"—Ripken was given a framed copy of the commemorative ticket used for the game. It read, "Farewell Cal Ripken" and had black-and-white pictures of Ripken and Gehrig.

Finally, on October 6, 2001, Ripken said goodbye to Baltimore and played his final game, No. 3,001 of his career. He arrived by himself at Camden Yards at 3:30 P.M. and met with his wife and two children in the clubhouse video room. Minutes later, the Orioles told him that the club would donate $1-million for the construction of a mini-Camden Yards at Ripken's youth baseball project in his hometown of Aberdeen, Maryland.

At four o'clock, Ripken walked into the clubhouse, spoke with his teammates and then headed to his locker to put on his playing uniform for the final time. In the dugout, he was surrounded by well-wishers and media and gave one interview after another.

"I've had my fill," Ripken said of his decision to retire.

"I know he's probably going to be relieved when it's over," teammate Brady Anderson said. "With a lot of athletes, you feel bad for them when they leave. They seem so sad, distraught or devastated. It's the opposite for Cal. I honestly think it's going to be a relief from the grind and the attention he has received. In that way, it won't be sad."

The pre-game ceremony honoring Ripken began at 6:12, and he was introduced to the crowd of 48,807, to a rousing ovation at 6:19. He stood on a stage with his wife, children and mother. Former President Bill Clinton was there. He called Ripken "the kind of man every father would like his son to grow up to be." Bud Selig was there, too, as was the Mayor of Baltimore and Orioles owner Peter Angelos. The mayor said Lee Street, near the stadium, would be renamed Ripken Way. The Orioles retired Ripken's No. 8. Ripken was given gifts—including a Waterford vase engraved with the likeness of Memorial Stadium, the Orioles' old home, and Camden Yards—and feted with superlatives, as he had been for most of his career. But when Angelos presented Ripken with a four-foot portrait of his father and former manager, Cal Ripken, Sr., Cal Jr. almost broke down.

"That was the most powerful thing to me," Ripken said. "It stared at me the whole time."

Selig announced that the Cal Ripken Jr. Award would be presented to any player who plays all of his team's games in any season.

Then, just when Ripken thought the ceremony was over and the game would begin, he was surprised to see that the entire starting lineup from his first Major League start in 1981 had taken its place on the field, including Weaver.

Ripken wasn't nearly as successful at the plate in his retirement game as he had been in the All-Star Game. In his first at-bat, he lined out to left. In his second at-bat, he popped to short.

The final at-bat of his career took place in the bottom of the eighth inning at 9:48 P.M. The crowd gave Ripken another standing ovation. He tipped his cap, exhaled, stepped into the batter's box, and waited for David Cone's first pitch. Two balls, then a foul. Flashbulbs were going off all over the stadium. Finally, Ripken swung and lofted a fly ball to centerfield. Trot Nixon settled under it and made the catch, then Ripken retreated to the dugout as the crowd continued to cheer. There was another curtain call, a wave of the hand and Ripken's verbal acknowledgment of the crowd: "That's all."

But the celebration wasn't over. After the game, Ripken climbed into a vintage convertible and circled the field. Confetti fell from the sky. Video of Ripken was shown on the warehouse wall. The stadium lights went off and Ripken walked to the microphone between third base and shortstop, the two positions he played.

"One question I've repeatedly been asked these last few weeks is how do I want to be remembered," Ripken said. "My answer has been simple: To be remembered at all is pretty special. I might also add that if I am remembered, I hope it's because by living my dream I was able to make a difference."

He would retire with one World Series championship, two All-Star Game MVP awards, two Gold Gloves, two MVPs, 19 All-Star Games and more than 3,000 hits and with the knowledge he had made an impact on many people because of his dedication and the way he carried himself.

Finally, fireworks exploded. A giant No. 8 burned against the centerfield wall. And Ripken disappeared into the dugout for the final time as a player, but certainly not for the final time of his life.

"I don't think I'll ever divorce myself from the game of baseball," Ripken said. "I don't see this as an ending. I see it as a beginning of an opportunity and a chance."

BARRY BONDS

THE NEW SULTAN OF SWAT WITH 73 HOME RUNS

Prior to the 2000 season, Barry Bonds of the San Francisco Giants had never hit more than 46 homeruns in a season. In 2000, he hit 49. In 2001, he turned 37 years old.

Before Mark McGwire set a Major League Record with 70 homers in 1998, he had never hit more than 58 in a season.

Roger Maris hit 61 homers in the 1961 season, but otherwise he never hit more than 39 in a season.

And then there's Babe Ruth, who hit 60 homeruns in 1927 after hitting 54 in 1920 and 59 in 1921.

In reality, there's only one homerun king in baseball history who didn't benefit from pitching deflation and offense inflation: The Babe.

But, as Bonds honed in on the homerun record, just three seasons after it was set, MLB Commissioner Bud Selig weighed in with the following sentiment: "It's a remarkable achievement. This is only three years since McGwire's record, but that can't distract from it. Everybody has had an opportunity, but only one person is doing it."

Indeed, in 2001, when Barry Bonds broke McGwire's homerun record with 73, the next closest slugger, Sammy Sosa of the Cubs, hit 64. In the American League, nobody had more than 52. In the era of inflation, Bonds was the one who found the most bargains.

So take that, Bonds critics. Yeah, The Babe might have hit a hundred homers against today's pitching, but The Babe isn't alive, Bonds is, and in 2001, he was as electric as any homerun hitter has ever been.

Love him or hate him—and a lot of people, especially those in the media, dislike Bonds intensely—his was the most memorable achievement in a season filled with memorable achievements. The homerun record is the king of North American sports records, and Bonds is its current owner.

But, even more than that, Bonds had perhaps the greatest season by any hitter in Major League history. In 2001, Bonds:

- Broke McGwire's homerun record with 73.
- Broke Babe Ruth's slugging percentage record with a .863 average.
- Broke Ruth's record for walks in a season with 177.
- Had a .515 on-base percentage, the highest in the National League since 1900.
- Tied Chuck Klein's 1930 National League record with 107 extra-base hits.
- Set the MLB record with 15.34 homers per 100 at-bats.
- Became the oldest player to lead the majors in homers.
- Became the oldest player to hit 50, 60 and 70 homers.
- Set the record with 39 homers before the All-Star break.
- Had two six-game homerun streaks, making him the only player to do so . . . in a career.
- Tied Frank Howard's 1968 record of eight homeruns in five games.
- Won a record fourth National League Most Valuable Player Award.

Need we go on? And he did all of this after a less-than-impressive start. Bonds hit his first homerun of the season in his third at-bat of the season, against San Diego Padres pitcher Woody Williams at Pac Bell Park in San Francisco. He then went homerless in six straight games—21 at-bats—before starting a six-game homer streak on April 12 in San Diego. On April 17 against Los Angeles at Pac Bell Park, with Willie Mays (his godfather) and Willie McCovey watching, Bonds struck his 500th career homer.

"I kind of got starstruck for a little while, a little nervous, trying to block things out of my mind and go back to the basic things and play the game, "Bonds said of the cold streak which preceded the hot streak. "It's hard to explain the feeling that you go through. It's like you never dreamt you'd be in a position to do certain things in your life and your career. You never thought it was possible or reachable. The next thing you find out, you're knocking on the door and you're a little bit nervous. You find you're on center stage. You're out there by yourself alone."

Of course, Bonds often felt alone. During the 1998 season, McGwire and his closest pursuer, Sammy Sosa, were cheered by the fans at every stop as they went after Maris's homerun record. But Bonds has never had many fans, other than former Pirates and Marlins manager Jim Leyland, and the 2001 homerun chase placed his personality under greater scrutiny. When Bonds hit his 500th homer, none of his teammates came out of the dugout to congratulate him.

He had always been viewed by his teammates as aloof, uncaring and conceited, and by the media as lazy and uncooperative. Barry who didn't run out grounders. Barry who didn't answer questions after games. Barry who twice didn't pose with his teammates for the team picture. Barry who stretched and worked out on his own. Barry who has three lockers in the Giants' clubhouse at Pac Bell Park.

"That's Barry," Giants second baseman Jeff Kent told *Sports Illustrated*. "He doesn't answer questions. He palms everybody off on us, so we have to do his talking for him. But you get used to it. Barry does a lot of questionable things. But you get used to it. Sometimes it rubs the younger guys the wrong way, and sometimes

it rubs the veterans the wrong way. You just hope he shows up for the game and performs. I've learned not to worry about it or think about it or analyze it. I was raised to be a team guy, and I am, but Barry's Barry. On the field, we're fine, but off the field, I don't care about Barry and Barry doesn't care about me. Or anybody else."

Bonds hit eleven homeruns in April, which put him on a pace close to McGwire, then obliterated McGwire's pace. He had his second six-game homerun streak from May 17-22 and hit three homeruns on May 19 in Atlanta. In ten at-bats at Turner Field on

May 18, 19 and 20, Bonds hit six solo homeruns, and Braves pitcher Jose Cabrera, who gave up the third homer, remembered his personal shelling very well.

"It's two-and-oh and I want to try to make the guy hit the ball," Cabrera said. "But, wow, I remember it right now, the sound it made when he hit that ball. I mean, I didn't even have to look back."

Said Giants manager Dusty Baker, "If I've seen it before, I don't remember it. He's hitting right-handers, left-handers. It doesn't matter."

Added Brian Jordan of the Braves, "That's the first time I've ever seen an individual performance like that. It just shows how great he is."

Bonds hit two homeruns on May 30 against Arizona to become the most prolific homerun left-handed homerun hitter in National League history. His 17 homeruns in May tied Ruth's record for most homers in a month by a lefty.

The homerun race wasn't even close. The eyes of the baseball world were turning to San Francisco, where McGwire's young record was clearly in jeopardy. At least everybody else thought it was. After hitting his 38th homerun of the season on June 20th in San Diego, Bonds stood in the clubhouse at Qualcomm Stadium and was asked whether he would break McGwire's record.

"Not a chance," he said. "The gut feeling in my heart: I don't think so. I'm not Mark McGwire. I'm just not that powerful a hitter. Mark is so much stronger than I am. The difference is, even when Mark is tired, the ball goes 520 feet. When I'm tired, or a normal guy is tired, it goes 230 feet. Mark hits the ball out of the park and we hit it to the shortstop. If someone was as big and strong as he was, I'd probably say that person has a chance. Mark can miss a ball and hit a homerun. We can't miss a ball and hit a homerun."

Bonds looked like a visionary when he hit his 39th homer in the first inning on June 23rd in St. Louis, then didn't hit another one until after the All-Star break: July 12 in Seattle. He would hit only six homers in July, giving him 45 with two months to play. Bonds

(Opposite page) Record breakers: When this picture was taken on June 22, 2001, Mark McGwire of the Cardinals was still the single-season homerun king with 70. Bonds didn't think he could catch McGwire, but he not only caught him, he passed him with 73 homers.

had seemingly run out of gas. He needed 25 homeruns just to tie McGwire's record, and opposing pitchers weren't exactly giving him good pitches to hit.

Meanwhile, he was doing everything he could to reinvent his image. The Giants were in a heated pennant race, and Bonds kept insisting that winning and getting his team to the playoffs was more important than hitting homers. Teammates noticed that he was becoming friendlier. He started giving more interviews and joking with reporters. He was acknowledging the fans after his homeruns.

"The more scrutiny, notoriety and pressure he was under this year, he became more open, and that's very uncommon for any athlete, especially for Barry, who's been a closed type person," said Kent, who was becoming a fan. "I think every week he became more open. He's been open with the media and open with teammates both in the locker room and on the field."

Said Giants shortstop Rich Aurilia: "I saw him smile a lot more than he did in the past."

Bonds, as is his way, had the opposite view. "I don't think I've changed at all," he said. "I think you guys [the media] are nicer, and with my teammates, we have fun. When you're doing so well, you're a part of it and the whole team is a part of it. There's joy with everyone."

Bonds hit 12 homers in August and entered September with 57 homers: 13 short of McGwire's mark. On September 9, Bonds hit three homers in Colorado against the Rockies, pushing him to 63.

"Barry is different now," Kent said. "He's swinging at more pitches and being more aggressive. When he goes to the plate, everybody is watching. We all know how hard it is to do what he's doing."

Said Arizona pitcher Curt Schilling, who allowed three of Bonds' homers, "I haven't seen him miss a pitch this year. The only thing I can compare him to is Matt Williams in '94. I felt Matt could sit the whole game waiting for one pitch, and when he got that pitch, he hit it out. Barry is the same, but I don't think it's one pitch. There are multiple pitches he can hit out. What's more amazing is that so many teams pitch around him, you would assume he mentally would get behind the eight-ball. He hasn't done that, which is a further testament to how great a hitter he is."

But there was nothing Bonds or anyone else could do on September 11, the date of the worst terrorist attack in U.S. history. When the season resumed on September 18, Bonds seemed distracted. He was hitless in two games against the Astros, then struck his 64th on September 20.

Fifteen games to go, six homers to tie.

He went two more games without a homer before hitting Nos. 65 and 66 in San Diego on September 23.

Twelve games remaining, four homers to tie.

"You could tell the last couple of days, he's pressing, trying to lift," said Tony Gwynn of the Padres, who helped Bonds with his swing before the game. "I just told him to keep doing what he's been doing. Don't let the pressure dictate what type of swing you take. It wasn't like I was giving him any secret things he didn't know about."

No. 67 came on September 24 in Los Angeles, but then he was walked four times in the last two games of the series and flew home three homers short with nine games to play.

Yet, tragedy awaited Bonds. Earlier in the summer, an uncle and a cousin had died, and on September 27, one of Bonds' closest friends and bodyguard for twelve years, Franklin Bradley, died unexpectedly from complications due to abdominal surgery. Bonds had paid for the surgery and took his friend's death hard.

The next night at Pac Bell Park, Bonds was somber—nothing really unusual—before the Giants' game against the Padres. Then, in the second inning, he hit a 438-foot solo homer that soared over the right-centerfield fence, and as he rounded the bases with No. 68, Bonds' emphatically pointed to the sky with both arms. When he reached the bench, he sat down and wept into his hands. During the post-game press conference, what had been a mundane question-and-answer session turned dramatic when a reporter asked Bonds about maintaining focus.

"One of my friends . . . I lost yesterday," Bonds said as tears welled and he choked up. And later he added, "Every time I have the

Barry Bonds celebrates and points to the sky to honor his friend, Franklin Bradley, after tying the Major League single-season homerun record with his 70th on October 4 in Houston. Bradley had died a week earlier.

| ONE FOR THE AGES: THE PLAYERS

opportunity to exhale or breathe, something has come up that has been difficult for me. I had a very disappointing article that came out, what happened with the [September 11] tragedy and some other issues, and I lose one of my best friends yesterday. Every time I want to enjoy it for a minute, something else happens. When I really want to give you guys the story I want, it seems like I just can't. I haven't had time."

But Bonds didn't have to take time out to tell a story in words. He was telling it through his actions. That same night, Bonds was walked twice to bring his season total to 164, breaking McGwire's previous National League record of 162.

And the story continued one night later, September 29, in San Francisco. Bonds ledoff the sixth inning against Padres pitcher Chuck McElroy and took ball one. After a swinging strike, Bonds worked the count to two-and-one, then sent McElroy's next pitch, a fastball, 437-feet away into San Francisco Bay for No. 69.

"I tried to get him out with the same pitch as always," McElroy said. "I wanted it outside, but it came back over. Now you can see it in his eyes. He's hungry and he's trying to get his team into the playoffs."

Bonds was in a much better mood on this night. He slapped hands with his teammates and grinned widely when he ran out to leftfield to start the seventh and received a standing ovation from the crowd.

"Yesterday, I did something for a friend, and I was able to let it go after that," Bonds said. "Today, go back to work, try to keep winning."

Said Padres manager Bruce Bochy: "It's not that easy to hit homeruns, and it's like he's playing in a Little League park right now. There's no way to get him out."

The countdown to 70 was in full force. Bonds was one homer away from tying McGwire with seven games remaining, including three in homer-friendly Enron Field in Houston. On Sunday afternoon, September 30, Pac Bell Park was packed with Giants fans hoping to witness history. McCovey Cove overflowed with rowboats, sailboats, rubber dinghies, canoes, kayaks and surfboards.

A giant seal mascot sat in a rubber raft. The fans gave Bonds a standing ovation each time he came to the plate and chanted his first name, but the Padres weren't going to allow themselves to be a footnote to history. In a 5-4 loss that damaged the Giants' playoff hopes, Bonds saw eleven pitches, but only one strike. He grounded out once, walked twice and was hit by a pitch.

"You have to pitch to him carefully," Padres starter Brian Tollberg said. "I didn't want to be in the record books, to be honest."

After a day off, Bonds brought the chase to Houston. In the first inning, with a runner on first and one out, Bonds was hit by a pitch by Shane Reynolds. In the fourth inning, he walked on five pitches, and all five pitches were reachable. In the sixth, Bonds singled up the middle. In the seventh, he was walked intentionally. And in the ninth inning, facing Billy Wagner, Bonds worked the count to three-and-one, then grounded out. For Bonds, the only positive of the night was that his team won, 4-1.

"You can't do anything if you're not pitched to," Bonds said after facing thirteen pitches by Reynolds and only two strikes. Then he continued working on reinventing his image. "You take what they give you. We won, that's all that matters. If I go back over the fifteen years I've been in baseball and look at all the pitchers I've faced, I'd say they've all had more success against me than I've had against them. I've probably faced 2,000 pitchers, but most of them have won more battles than I have. I may have hit a homerun to win a game against somebody, but I also probably went one-for-four and they got me out three times, too. So they've won more battles."

Right, Barry. The next night, with Willie Mays watching, Bonds's opponent was righty Tim Redding, who vowed to go after Bonds. In the first inning, Bonds faced all fastballs in the mid-90s and went down swinging. In the fourth inning, he walked on four pitches. In the sixth inning against righty Nelson Cruz, Bonds again walked on four pitches. His 171st walk of the season broke Babe Ruth's Major League record set in 1923. He was intentionally walked in the seventh, and Bonds' two daughters held up a sign that read, "Pitch to Our Daddy." Bonds singled in the eighth, but he had now gone three games without a homer.

BARRY BONDS CAREER STATISTICS

- ✦ Height: 6'2"
- ✦ Weight: 210 lbs.
- ✦ Throws: Left
- ✦ Bats: Left
- ✦ Born: July 24, 1964, Riverside, California

SEASON	TEAM	G	AB	R	H	2B	3B	HR	RBI	BB	SO	SB	CS	OBP	SLG	OPS	AVG
1986	PITTSBURGH	113	413	72	92	26	3	16	48	65	102	36	7	.330	.416	.746	.223
1987	PITTSBURGH	150	551	99	144	34	9	25	59	54	88	32	10	.329	.492	.821	.261
1988	PITTSBURGH	144	538	97	152	30	5	24	58	72	82	17	11	.368	.491	.859	.283
1989	PITTSBURGH	159	580	96	144	34	6	19	58	93	93	32	10	.351	.426	.777	.248
1990	PITTSBURGH	151	519	104	156	32	3	33	114	93	83	52	13	.406	.565	.971	.301
1991	PITTSBURGH	153	510	95	149	28	5	25	116	107	73	43	13	.410	.514	.924	.292
1992	PITTSBURGH	140	473	109	147	36	5	34	103	127	69	39	8	.456	.624	1.080	.311
1993	SAN FRANCISCO	159	539	129	181	38	4	46	123	126	79	29	12	.458	.677	1.135	.336
1994	SAN FRANCISCO	112	391	89	122	18	1	37	81	74	43	29	9	.426	.647	1.073	.312
1995	SAN FRANCISCO	144	506	109	149	30	7	33	104	120	83	31	10	.431	.577	1.008	.294
1996	SAN FRANCISCO	158	517	122	159	27	3	42	129	151	76	40	7	.461	.615	1.076	.308
1997	SAN FRANCISCO	159	532	123	155	26	5	40	101	145	87	37	8	.446	.585	1.031	.291
1998	SAN FRANCISCO	156	552	120	167	44	7	37	122	130	92	28	12	.438	.609	1.047	.303
1999	SAN FRANCISCO	102	355	91	93	20	2	34	83	73	62	15	2	.389	.617	1.006	.262
2000	SAN FRANCISCO	143	480	129	147	28	4	49	106	117	77	11	3	.440	.688	1.128	.306
2001	SAN FRANCISCO	153	476	129	156	32	2	73	137	177	93	13	3	.515	.863	1.378	.328
CAREER TOTALS		2296	7932	1713	2313	483	71	567	1542	1724	1282	484	138	.419	.585	1.004	.292

Bonds charged that the Astros were afraid of him, but Redding countered, "If he thinks we're cowardly for walking him, maybe he's a little high on himself. We're not out here to set major league records, we're here to win ballgames. The fans are here to see something special. I'd like to see if he could do it, too. But I'm not a guy that's going to give it to him. He's got to earn it."

Now the pressure was really on. Only four games remained.

Game 159. October 4, Enron Field. The Astros walked Bonds three times in the game, including intentionally in the sixth inning when they were trailing 8-1, enraging the Giants.

"[First-base coach] Robby Thompson was really upset because it wasn't a close game," Bonds said. "Everyone could understand if the

situation was a close game. After that, I just went in the dugout and said, 'You know, it's tough being this patient.'"

Like he had a choice. Bonds would've needed a tree branch to reach some of the pitches the Astros were throwing him. But, in the ninth inning, Bonds finally found a challenger. Unknown reliever Wilfredo Rodriguez pitching. Giants leading, 9-2. Bonds led off the inning, and Rodriguez threw a high fastball. Bonds swung and missed.

"I was like, 'Wow,'" Bonds said. "It's rare to see a lefty throw as hard as Billy Wagner or Randy Johnson. He doesn't throw *that* hard, but he's close."

The next pitch was another high fastball. Bonds laid off for ball one. Another fastball. Bonds swung and made direct contact. The ball took off, like something Roy Hobbs might have struck in *The Natural*. Bonds knew the ball was gone. He dropped his bat, watched the ball's arc, and raised his arms. The ball kept going, and going, before landing 454 feet away in the upper deck in right-centerfield. The sellout crowd would've been in awe even if it hadn't been Bonds' record-tying 70th homer, but, of course, it was. He laughed and smiled as he rounded the bases. He pointed to the sky for his friend Franklin Bradley when he touched homeplate and was greeted by his teammates. He hugged his son, Nikolai.

"I just feel grateful to share something with someone that I have a lot of respect for," Bonds said, speaking of McGwire. "I just feel proud to be on the same level with Mark. He put the homerun record where it is."

The historic ball was caught by a man named Charles Murphy, who enthused, "I felt the ball hit my hand and I pulled it out. That was a rush of energy and then a miraculous rush of estrogen or whatever it was. It was a moment of glory I could not let go. And they thought Jesus was coming because I was telling them, 'Jesus was coming.'"

The fans, including Barry's father, Bobby, and Willie Mays, cheered Bonds as if he was a member of the home team, and not one of the most hated players in baseball. Bonds made two curtain calls, and when he ran out to leftfield for the bottom of the ninth, he was greeted by the Giants' relievers.

(Opposite page) A moment in history: Bonds connects off of knuckleballer Dennis Springer of the Dodgers on October 7 at Pac Bell Park to establish the new single-season homerun record: 73.

"Home plate was good, but when the guys came from the bullpen, that touched me even more," Bonds said.

So Bonds came home with a share of the record and three games remaining to establish his own mark. There was another sellout crowd. More anticipation. And a final weekend with the Giants still in the playoff race, but barely.

September 5. Pac Bell Park. The opponent was the hated Los Angeles Dodgers, who earlier in the season had been the victims of Bonds's 500th career homer and had been angry when the Giants interrupted the game for a brief ceremony.

Bonds wasn't in the happiest of moods. The team had arrived home from Houston at three a.m. that morning, and he had attended his friend's funeral. During his pre-game press conference, when asked if hitting his 70th homer had sunk in, Bonds said. "I really haven't had a chance to enjoy it. I had to put to rest a friend of mine today."

The Giants were trailing, 5-0, in the bottom of the first inning when Bonds came to bat against Chan Ho Park. The crowd rose. Flashbulbs went off everywhere as Park missed outside and low on the first pitch for ball one. The stadium clock showed 8:15. Bonds swung at the next pitch and connected. Like the record-tying homer, this one got out of the park in a hurry, 442-feet away in right-centerfield for his record-breaking 71st homerun.

Unlike his display after his 70th homer, Bonds didn't show much excitement. After all, his team was trailing badly in a critical game. He watched the ball clear the fence and trotted around the bases. When he crossed home plate, he pointed skyward again in his friend's honor, and picked up Nikolai. Bonds' teammates gathered around him. The fans got one curtain call. In the dugout, Barry took a phone call from his father, who was hosting a golf tournament in Connecticut. He ran over to the seats behind the backstop to hug his wife and mother. Fireworks went off. Two massive banners were unfurled on either side of the scoreboard, one reading "Bonds," the other reading "71."

The record didn't last long. In the bottom of the third, with the Giants trailing, 8-4, Bonds went to one-and-one against Park, then deposited his 72nd homerun over the centerfield fence. Again, Bonds showed little excitement. He rounded the bases routinely. He signaled to his friend. He picked up Nikolai.

But, at the end of the night, the Giants lost the longest nine-inning game in history, 11-10, and were eliminated from the playoffs.

"You can't dampen what Barry did just because we lost to the Dodgers or didn't win the wild card," Kent said, now a Bonds rooter like everyone else. "Barry has been great this year and over achieved while pushing this team. He should be very proud. He's been telling you guys all year that all he wants to do is win. I'm sure just like all of us, he is disappointed we couldn't beat the Dodgers tonight."

After the long, disappointing game ended, the Giants honored Bonds with a post-game ceremony. A sign was erected on the field reading, "Barry Bonds 71 Homeruns," but, of course, that sign was already outdated. The fans chanted "Barry, Barry!" and Bonds was brought to tears.

"We've come a long way," he told the crowd. "We've had our ups and downs. Thank you."

With the Giants eliminated, Bonds pinch-hit in Game 161 and didn't hit a homer. In the first inning of Game 162, Bonds homered off knuckleball pitcher Dennis Springer for No. 73 . . . the new single-season homerun record.

"I was just in shock," Bonds said. "The chance of hitting a homerun off a guy who throws that slow is slim. I just said, 'What else can you give me, God? Enough is enough.'"

Enough? Bonds had been piling on all season. Besides breaking the homerun record, Bonds finished with a .515 on-base percentage, the highest in the National League since John McGraw's .547 in 1899. Bonds also set a major-league record by hitting one homerun every 6.52 at-bats. His slugging percentage of .863 destroyed Babe Ruth's previous record .847 set in 1920.

"That's the one I think is not going to be broken," Bonds said. "I wouldn't be surprised if someone breaks 73. I don't know if that record will still exist next year. But this was a great, great way to end it with a victory and a homerun. You can't ask for anything better. I never thought I could do it."

"Soon the Babe's not going to have any records, is he?" Dusty Baker said. "I think it's awesome. This was one of the greatest years, no, it was the greatest year I have seen from a single person."

"What can I say about Barry Bonds?" Dodgers manager Jim Tracy said. "He had a tremendous season, the way that he handled everything. If he had been pitched to on a constant basis, he might have hit a hundred homeruns."

In baseball these days, the sky's the limit. But, for now, the sky belongs to Barry Bonds.

MIGHTY MAC RETIRES

WE THOUGHT WE WERE LOSING only two first-ballot Hall of Famers, Tony Gwynn and Cal Ripken, Jr., during the 2001 season, but we ended up losing a third, too: In mid-November, Mark McGwire, the single-season homerun king until Barry Bonds came along this year, faxed in his retirement . . . to ESPN.

"I am walking away from the game that has proved me opportunities, experiences, memories and friendships to fill ten lifetimes," wrote McGwire, who had agreed to a contract extension, but never signed the contract. "After considerable discussion with those closest to me, I have decided not to sign the extension, as I am unable to perform at a level equal to the salary the organization would be paying me. I believe I owe it to the Cardinals and the fans of St. Louis to step aside so a talented free agent can be brought in as the final piece of what I expect can be a world championship-caliber team."

The Cardinals were stunned that McGwire hadn't told them first, but by the next day, he had faxed his retirement plans to the team and the *St. Louis Post-Dispatch*, too.

The Cardinals weren't surprised about the information, though. When the season ended, McGwire had spoken to St. Louis general manager Walt Jocketty and told him the 2001 season had been his last.

"Before he left St. Louis to go home, we had a meeting and he told me he was going to retire," Jocketty said. "He had a lot of self-doubts about what he could do. I told him to think about it and call me when he decided how and when he wanted to handle it."

After hitting 70 homers in 1998 and 65 in 1999, a sore right knee had plagued McGwire, 38, over the past two seasons. He dipped to 32 homers in 89 games in 2000, then hit 29 homers in 97 games last season while batting only .187. McGwire had first suggested he might retire in early July, then backtracked. Later in the season, he talked about how his mind and body were worn down from the pressures and demands of playing.

In his final at-bat, in Game Five of the National League Division Series in Arizona, McGwire struckout swinging. Then, in the ninth inning, Cardinals manager Tony LaRussa pinch-hit for McGwire with the game tied, a move that would have been unheard of a few years earlier.

"One of my lowest moments as a manager was pinch-hitting for Mark," LaRussa said. "It's not something I'm going to remember fondly."

McGwire's final record: In 2001, he became the third player in Major League history to hit more than 20 homers and bat less than .200. He struckout 118 times in only 299 at-bats. Clearly, the giant had been felled by his bad knee. But history will be far kinder to McGwire. It will recall his 583 career homeruns and his electrifying 1998 run for the record, which revitalized a game badly in need of revitalization.

Said Cardinals rookie Albert Pujols, "It [his retirement] shocked me. I said, 'Oh, my God.' I couldn't believe it. I heard a lot of rumors, but I never thought it was going to happen. It was an honor to play with Mark McGwire this year. He took care of me and helped me out a lot. He helped me relax. I saw how he approached the game, how he reacted when he made a mistake or how he reacted when he had a bad at-bat."

"For years, I have said my motivation for playing wasn't for fame and fortune, but rather the love of competing," McGwire said in the statement. "Baseball is a team sport and I have been lucky enough to contribute to the success of some great teams."

McGwire, along with Ripken and Gwynn, are sure to be first-ballot Hall of Famers when they become eligible in 2007. What a ceremony that's going to be.

THE TEAMS

11

SEATTLE MARINERS
SUPERSTARS? WHO NEEDS SUPERSTARS?

THE GREATEST SEASON in American League history didn't come without planning. First, the Mariners had to get rid of lefthanded fireballer Randy Johnson. His wins and strikeouts had made him too ritzy for the Mariners' small-market bankroll. Seattle jettisoned him to the Arizona Diamondbacks during the 1998 season, and he went on to win three Cy Young Awards in a row.

The master plan was in motion.

Next to go: outfielder Ken Griffey Jr. He had hit 49, 56, 56 and 48 homers in four seasons, which meant he was too expensive for a team with Burger King tastes. Junior forced a trade to Cincinnati after the 1999 season and hit 40 homers the next.

Hey, who needed him?

Finally, because they absolutely, positively had to make sure they didn't have any superstars in their lineup, they told Alex Rodriguez, the best all-around shortstop in baseball, that he could take his big bat elsewhere. So he did, to the Texas Rangers, who happened to play in the same division, the American League West, as the Mariners.

What, we worry? seemed to be the Mariners' attitude.

Really, why worry? With their franchise players gone, the Mariners played their third season at Safeco Field without a marquee player on their marquee. Instead, they had this:

Rightfielder Ichiro Suzuki, the first Japanese-born position player in the Major Leagues, who batted 692 times in the leadoff spot, hit .350 in his first Major League season and became only the second American Leaguer to win Rookie of the Year and Most Valuable Player in the same year. Ho-hum.

"Of course I am amazed myself," Suzuki said, not sounding amazed at all as Mariners fans traded in their A-Rod jerseys for Ichiro models. "When I look back from where I started, I didn't think of any numbers to achieve."

Which made him right at home: neither did the rest of his teammates.

They had second baseman Bret Boone, who batted .331—76 points over his career average—and hit 37 homers, including 36 as a second baseman, the most by any American League pivot man in history.

"It's about the right time in his career for him to come together, mentally and physically," Mariners manager Lou Piniella said of his 32-year-old sudden-star, who fielded worth a damn, too. "He's matured a lot as a player. He's tempered his cockiness a bit. He's more selective than when we had him before. He's learned the strike zone, and he puts the ball in play."

They had designated hitter Edgar Martinez, a Mariner since his career began in 1987 (poor guy, you once might've said), who batted .306 with 116 RBIs, and quietly went about his business of being the second-best hitter on the team . . . and the highest-paid Mariner ever (no, not A-Rod, not Junior, not The Big Unit, but Martinez).

"He isn't your typical superstar," Boone said. "His attitude won't tell you that, but his stats say he is. Sometimes, you tell him how much you like to watch him hit, and it's like he's embarrassed. In today's game, once you get to a certain level, it's like you're expected to act a different. Edgar doesn't do that."

They had first baseman John Olerud, the picture of consistency, who returned to the .300-zone he once inhabited regularly by hitting .302 with 95 RBIs and making his former team, the Mets, think, *Wish we still had him.*

And they had pitching. Freddy Garcia, who went 18-6 and led the American League with a 3.05 ERA, proved that his 17 wins in 1999, his rookie season, weren't a fluke. The six-foot-five Garcia dominated with his overhand curve and struckout 163 in 238 innings. Not Johnson numbers, but awfully good.

"That's got to be difficult, hitting against him," Mariners starter Paul Abbott said. "He's six-foot-five and he really gets his arm up there over his head. The pitch comes at you hard, then it breaks fast. It's something special to watch."

They had lefthander Jamie Moyer, also no Johnson, but the ace of the Seattle staff with 20 wins and a 3.43 ERA, a guy who rebounded strong from 13-10, 5.39 ERA the year before to become, at age 38, the oldest American Leaguer to win 20 games for the first time. In the Year of the Geezer (Bonds, Clemens, etc.), Moyer was the Mariners' Old Guy of the Year.

Veteran Aaron Sele went 15-5. The Mariners' four-man rotation of Moyer, Garcia, Abbott (17-4) and Sele rivaled the great starting rotations of all-time, including the 1986 Mets (Doc Gooden, Bobby Ojeda, Ron Darling and Sid Fernandez) and the 1971 Orioles (Mike Cuellar, Dave McNally, Pat Dobson and Jim Palmer). Closer Kaz Sasaki set a club record with 45 saves and a Major League record for saves in April with 13. Arthur Rhodes went 8-0 out of the bullpen. Jeff Nelson came over from the Yankees and continued to be perhaps the best setup man in baseball. Mark McLemore played six positions and batted from two sides. And Jay Buhner, who couldn't play because of a bad foot, contributed with his presence alone.

"He's still here," Abbott said. "If his name wasn't over his locker, there would be a big void in this clubhouse. He's like a security blanket."

Yeah, security blanket. Just what this team needed. And there was no void, not even one named Rodriguez or Johnson or Griffey.

After making it to the American League Championship Series in 2000, the Mariners could hardly be considered late-comers, but look at the players they've lost over the past three years and look at what they did. The Oakland A's were supposed to run away with the American League West, and the Rangers with A-Rod were given a shot, but the Mariners left every team in their wake.

They set an American League record with 116 wins. They spent every day of the season in first place. They won or tied their first 24 road series of the season. They sprinted out to an early lead, winning 20 games in April, and never looked back. How impressive were they? Well, the A's won 100 games—good enough to win the pennant in any other year, or in any other division in baseball—but the 116-46 Mariners still beat them by fourteen games.

The Mariners were an ungodly 47-12 in early June and 63-24 at the All-Star break. They won 15 straight games from May 23 through June 8 to take a 17-game lead over the California Angels. Basically, by mid-June, they had locked up a playoff berth, turning the rest of the season into a walkover. They were like Secretariat in the 1973 Belmont Stakes, in a league of their own, running off on their own . . . at least during the regular season.

And they did it by playing as a team. They didn't beat themselves at the plate, they didn't beat themselves on the mound, they didn't beat themselves in the field or on the bases. Only four Major League teams have won a greater percentage of their games in a single season: the 1906 Chicago Cubs (.763), 1902 Pittsburgh Pirates (.741), 1909 Pittsburgh Pirates (.724) and the 1954 Cleveland Indians (.721). Before the Mariners' four-game losing streak in September, they hadn't lost even three games in a row all season.

About the only people who weren't stunned by the Mariners were the Mariners, or so they said. Ballplayers, you know, typically say the opposite of what the media is saying. David Bell, who joined the team in 1998 a month after Johnson left and then watched Griffey and A-Rod depart, too, declared during spring training, "There's too much going on, too many guys in here with good talent to dwell on that. They're gone and there's not a whole lot you can do about it. As good a player as Alex is, he's only one player and this is by far the

Manager Lou Piniella and Mike Cameron raise the flag—the American flag—after the Mariners clinched first place in the American League West on September 19 with a 5-0 win over the Angels at Safeco Field in Seattle. The season had resumed on September 17 following the 9/11 terrorist attacks, and the Mariners wanted to celebrate as respectfully as possible in deference to those who died.

biggest team game there is in team sports. I feel like we can be better than we were last year. That's how important 25 guys on our roster are, not just one guy."

Yeah, right, David.

But, of course, he was right.

A-Rod returned to Seattle in mid-April, got booed out of the ballpark and was overshadowed by Ichiro as the Mariners took two out of three. Something was happening here.

"Suzuki's a lot better player than we saw in spring training," Billy Beane, Oakland's general manager, said. "Each time I see him he gets better and better. He's had a big impact on that club. They've been a little bit surprising, but I think Suzuki was always the wild card and he's turned out to be a pretty good player. The starters get them to the bullpen, and the bullpen is the best in baseball. If they've got you by two runs in the sixth inning, they can slam the door on you right there."

Sasaki was joined in the bullpen by Rhodes, Jose Paniagua, Ryan Franklin and veterans Norm Charlton and Nelson, who a year earlier was shutting down opponents as a middle reliever in the Yankees bullpen. Best bullpen in baseball? Did somebody forget about Mariano Rivera and the Yankees? Guess so.

"They've put the losses behind them," Rangers general manager Doug Melvin said. "The losses of Griffey and Randy Johnson might have prepared them for the loss of Alex. They were mentally prepared at that point."

Said Mariners general manager Pat Gillick, the man who—*ahem*—built the Mariners: "We've got a lot of people who from a character standpoint fit in, a lot of blue-collar guys. But we are not a small-market team. I'd call us a high-end mid."

Indeed, the Mariners didn't come cheap. Their payroll of $80-million was only $25-million less than the Yankees. They turned a $14.2-million profit in the 2000 season. Seats behind the plate at Safeco Field cost $195. Bargain-basement Mariners? Not exactly. Last remnants of old-time baseball? Not quite. *Forbes* magazine estimated that the Mariners are worth $323 million. Loveable small-market team-gone-good? Well, they did shell out $31-million—

$13-million to his old Japanese team and $18-million for the player—to get Ichiro.

"The game is not a precise game, but you try to be precise," Gillick said. "The difference between New York and Seattle is that New York can afford a mistake. We can't."

Wasn't getting rid of Johnson, A-Rod and Griffey supposed to be a mistake?

"Nothing Pat does surprises me," Yankees GM Brian Cashman said. "He wins everywhere he goes. He's the architect of all architects."

An architect who would say, "This big picture window facing the ocean has to go, let's replace it with a brick wall," then proceeds to get a higher price for the property.

"We got Ichiro before Alex left, but anticipating that Alex would go," Gillick said. "After Alex left, we signed Boone. The two surprises offensively for us have been the leadoff hitter [Ichiro] and Boone. We were short last year offensively, and we were concerned we were going to be short again. But Ichiro and Boone have made up for a lot of it."

"They lost Junior and everyone said they'd be in trouble," Yankees manager Joe Torre said. "But they shored themselves up with pitching. I look at that first."

"This is a team sport; it always has been," Tampa Bay Devil Rays general manager Chuck LeMar said. "You play with 25 players. It's been proven that one player in our sport truly does not make a difference in a championship club, unless he's the last piece of the puzzle. If there are two teams in baseball that exemplify that, it's the Seattle Mariners and the New York Yankees. They do the little things, play fundamental baseball and do it the right way. But don't get me wrong. It's not like the cupboard's dry and they're doing it on attitude. They've got some very good players over there."

On April 11 in Oakland, Ichiro made a 200-foot throw from rightfield to nail a runner trying to score, and Aaron Sele allowed only four hits in a 3-0 win. On April 16, the Mariners were 9-3 when A-Rod came to town and suggested his former team could win 115 games.

"They have the complete package," he said, sounding generous, not serious. But the Mariners were 20-4 after beating the White Sox, 8-5, on April 28.

"If you had told me in spring training that we'd be 20-4, I'd have said, 'I don't think so,'" Boone said. "Hey, it's a great run, let's ride it. This has been as impressive a run as I've ever seen. We feel like we're going to win every night."

They rode it. They won just about every night. They won eight in a row in mid-May to go 31-9. On May 31, Sele beat the Orioles, 2-1, to improve his record to eight wins, no losses; best ever by a Seattle pitcher. With a 40-12 record, the Mariners took a 14-game lead in the West into June.

"The biggest key to my start is that our club is doing so well," Sele said. "This is pretty nice."

"There are no hidden secrets," Moyer said. "It's not like we found out how to do it and we're just not telling anyone. We pitch good, we play good defense and we don't make a lot of mistakes."

After losing only five games in April, the Mariners lost only seven in May.

"When we won 20 in April and again in May, that's when I knew we had something special going here," Piniella said. "We built up the lead to five or six. Then we got it up to 10 or 12. Then it was 15, 20. And we did it in such a short period of time. We didn't just maintain it. We've played very well throughout. Who would have dreamed at the beginning of the season, that this team—or any team—would win 116 ballgames? It's almost incomprehensible."

The Mariners couldn't believe it, either. Before each home game, several players would stand in the outfield joking around and watching as the Major League standings were posted on the scoreboard. They loved the look of things.

"They show the division standings on the scoreboard and ours comes up last," Abbott said. "I pay attention. I want to see it. It doesn't come around like this every hundred years. It's like Halley's Comet. It doesn't look right."

It continued. The 15-game winning streak, the longest in the

American League in ten years, made the Mariners 47-12 and had people mentioning them in the same breath as the best teams in baseball history. The Mariners were on pace to finish 130-32 and had matched the 1907 Chicago Cubs for the second-best 59-game start since 1900, trailing only the 1912 New York Giants (48-11).

"They've surprised the baseball world with what they have done up to this point," San Diego Padres Bruce Bochy said after the Mariners disposed of his team. "It's hard to believe. I don't care how good you are, to have the record they have playing on the road and at home, I don't think anybody saw that coming."

On July 6 in Los Angeles, Garcia took a no-hitter into the sixth inning of a 13-0 win over the Dodgers. Two days later, the Mariners finished the first half with a 9-2 win over the Dodgers and a 63-24 record. And on July 10, the All-Star Game was played at Safeco Field, and a third of the Mariners were in the American League dugout: Ichiro, Sasaki, Garcia, Mike Cameron, Boone, Martinez, Olerud and Nelson. Ichiro ledoff the game with a hit. Garcia got the win. Sasaki got the save. Cameron, who was traded for Griffey Jr., turned a single into a double with hustle.

"I think it was great for what's going on in the city this year, for how well we've done in the first half," Boone said. "What epitomized it was to see the look on Mike Cameron's face and how excited he was."

What could the Mariners do for an encore? Win more games. On July 26 against Kansas City, rookie righthander Joel Pineiro retired 18 of the first 19 hitters he faced in a 4-0 victory. No, this team wasn't only about Ichiro, Garcia, Boone and the rest of the all-stars. On any night, any player was capable of performing like a hero. And when the Mariners beat the Twins, 10-2, on July 29, they were an amazing 76-29.

"You can't have the same nine guys contribute day-in and day-out," Ed Sprague said. "You're going to need the bench to step up on those other nights. Someone always seems to come up big for this team."

"Role players are what makes a team function like we have this year," Piniella said. "We're not deep, but we're experienced and they know how to prepare themselves for the game."

And the beating went on. Four straight wins to start August, then another four-game winning streak. No losing streaks of any kind. On August 17th at Yankee Stadium in New York, Jeff Nelson got his World Series ring and Cameron, admiring the jewelry, said, "It's a little reminder of what we're playing for." Then the Mariners took two straight from the world champions after losing the opener, with Cameron homering twice in the finale.

"I don't think we needed to prove anything," Boone said. "We've proven it all year."

Now, all that was left were the formalities. On September 3, the Mariners beat the Devil Rays, 3-2, in extra innings to clinch a playoff berth. Seattle became the fastest team to clinch a playoff berth since 1998, when the New York Yankees earned a playoff spot in their 134th game on August 29.

"Our ambitions are more than just making the playoffs," Piniella said.

On September 19, the third day after Major League Baseball resumed following the September 11 terrorist attacks, the Mariners beat the Angels, 5-0, at Safeco Field to clinch the West. They celebrated quietly, respectfully,

"One of the great things about this team is that nobody has been talking about next year or their next contract," Moyer said. "Nobody talks about the postseason, until now. Nobody talks about tomorrow's game. The talk is all about today."

Still, there were two more records to break: first, the 1998 Yankees' American League standard of 114 wins in a season. On October 4, the Mariners got their 114th win with a 16-1 victory over the Texas Rangers—A-Rod's team—at Safeco Field.

"I hope people realize what we just did," said Nelson, who was also a member of the 1998 Yankees. "A few years ago, this was a team in the Northwest that nobody would have heard of without Ken Griffey Jr. Now, it's won 114 games. Maybe it will win 117 games. Who knows?"

"I think the records are pushing us," backup catcher Tom

Lampkin said. "Guys are busting their behinds like it's April and May. We don't want to let up."

They didn't. The next night, the Mariners got No. 115 with a 6-2 win over Texas, and when the game ended, the sellout crowd gave its team a standing ovation.

"This is pretty darn special, isn't it?" Piniella said. "This only comes around once in a lifetime."

Said Yankees manager Joe Torre: "I said somebody would hit 80 homers before somebody would break our record."

Boone hit a two-run homer. Moyer won his 20th game.

"It's pretty awesome to be part of this," Moyer said. "To win 20 games for the first time on a night your team wins its 115th game is very special. It's something I'll hold onto for the rest of my life."

On October 6th, the Mariners beat the Rangers, 1-0, for their 116th win, tying the 1906 Cubs for the Major League record (the Cubs went 116-36 with three ties). They had one game left to break the record.

"I've never been too much of a baseball history buff, but I'm more in tune now," Piniella said, admitting he had been unaware of the record when the season began. "Look, it's a very nice accomplishment to say the least. It's a lot of wins."

"This is pretty cool," Boone said. "We've got one more win to go for the record. Of course, you want it. I thought we were a very good team coming out of spring training, but it doesn't matter how good you are. You can't envision something like this."

"A part of me says I feel like part of me won 116 games, too, because this was a three-year process," Alex Rodriguez said. "They had a great team last year. They just got the missing pieces."

But, in what might have been an omen of things to come, the Mariners finally fell short of something. In the final game of the regular season, the Mariners lost to the Rangers, 4-3, on an RBI single by Rafael Palmiero in the ninth inning.

"I'm sure everyone here knows this opportunity doesn't come around very often," Edgar Martinez said. "But it's still been a great year, and we're still in the record books."

"They have the greatest manager I've ever seen, leadership and the best bullpen I've seen," Rodriguez said.

He sounded like a jealous man, but, in fact, he was merely a player appreciating an outstanding team that had a once-in-a-century season. In winning two more games than the 1998 Yankees, the Mariners traveled more and played a slightly tougher schedule: they played the A's, the second-best team in the American League, 19 times. Their interleague games were against the National League West (home of the Arizona Diamondbacks and Barry Bonds's San Francisco Giants). And they didn't have any expansion teams to pick on, like the Yankees had.

Of course, the 1998 Yankees didn't lose their three best players in the three years leading up to their record season. The Mariners did everything against all odds.

"We got after it hard, one through nine, every night," Piniella said. "To think that a team could go through the entire season winning seven out of every ten games they played, to get the AL road record for wins with 59 and the all-time win record in the American League, that only comes around once in a lifetime."

"From a team aspect, it may never get better," Boone said. "We may never see another season like this."

Well, let's see what the 2002 season holds for them. During the off-season, the Mariners lost Sele to free-agency.

Look out, world.

12

NEW YORK METS
PLAYING FOR A MIRACLE

The New York Mets were in Pittsburgh on the morning of September 11, when two planes were crashed into the World Trade Center, one was crashed into the Pentagon and one was crashed into a field eighty miles outside of Pittsburgh. They had just finished winning three of four games against the Marlins in Florida and were hoping to continue their late-season resurgence, but all that changed in a flash.

As a security measure, the Mets, who were staying in a hotel next to a federal building in downtown Pittsburgh, were moved to a hotel outside the city. That day, as the nation reeled from a tragedy that would claim over 3,000 lives in New York City, Washington D.C. and Pennsylvania, all Major League Baseball games were called off for only the third time in history.

"I pray baseball can be part of the healing process," MLB Commissioner Bud Selig said. "But it's got to be done with only the healing considered, nothing else. We have a lot of responsibility. But above all, we have a responsibility to act in a way I think is befitting to a marvelous social institution. We're just a small part of society. Today is not a day to worry about the games. It's a day to worry about the World Trade Center and Washington."

The September 11 terrorist attacks were as unthinkable for the Mets as they were for everyone else. Multi-millionaires who work in a fantasy world were touched by real life. Superstar catcher Mike Piazza, who had moved back to Manhattan this season after living in northern New Jersey, lived several blocks north of the World Trade Center and could see the buildings from his apartment window.

"I can't imagine what that must be like now with it gone," he said. "I had a friend who was there. He called me. He said he had gotten away. He was all the way to the Brooklyn Bridge when one of the towers collapsed. He could feel a rumble in his feet. I can't imagine that." Playing baseball had become secondary to a person who was used to doing nothing else in September. "It's going to take a long time to recapture the feeling we had," he said, "to feel emotional about sports again, if you're watching or playing."

John Franco, a native New Yorker, reported that his son's Little League coach, a fireman, died at the World Trade Center. And the Mets found themselves at the center of attention, not only because they were among the most famous people in the city, but because Shea Stadium was transformed into a staging area for police, firefighters and emergency medical technicians. As more games were postponed—six in all for the Mets—a decision was made to move the Mets' scheduled September 17-19 series against the Pirates from Shea to Pittsburgh, both as a security measure and as a show of respect for those who died in the World Trade Center. And the Mets did what they could to help.

When the team got home, manager Bobby Valentine helped haul and organize food and clothing in the Shea Stadium parking lot. Several Mets worked long hours on the trucks gathered in the lot. Some of them visited hospitals in Manhattan. At two hospitals, injured policemen and firefighters rejected visits from dignitaries and welcomed the Mets.

"This," third baseman Robin Ventura said, "is what we can do."

But the Mets found out that they could do something else, too. They could entertain at a time when the city needed a diversion. They could give people something to rally around. They could play baseball and inspire.

The Mets had been the hottest team in baseball prior to September 11. After a terrible first four and a half months of the season, they were 54-68 and 13½ games out of first place after losing their seventh straight game, 8-3 to Los Angeles, on August 17. But the Mets went 10-3 for the rest of August and were 7-2 in September, just eight games behind first-place Atlanta, when the season was interrupted. Still, only eighteen games remained for the Mets to pull off a miracle.

Valentine remained at Shea Stadium to help the relief effort long after the rest of the team had departed for Pittsburgh the day before the season re-opener. "I'm not sure what else I could have done," he said. "We provide entertainment, and entertainment is always about getting away from the seriousness of life. I hope we're helping. I think we are."

About 10,000 fans showed up in Pittsburgh on September 17 for the resumption of normal life, but there was nothing normal about what happened that night. A bedsheet hung above the bleachers at PNC Park reading, "NYC, USA, We are family. Pgh. Pa." Fans waved flags and wore "I Love New York" buttons. Mets coach Mookie Wilson reflected the feelings of many when he discussed the sudden outpouring of affection for New Yorkers.

"I came from the South," he said. "I had the impression that New York was distant and everyone was selfish. The more you're in New York, you find out New Yorkers are some of the most caring people in America. This is in our house."

There really was no visiting team on this night, just two American baseball teams trying to return to business as usual when everything was anything but usual. The fans cheered as the Mets and Pirates lined up on the foul lines as if it was opening day. The Mets wore caps from the fire department, police department, and emergency services of the City of New York. Bishop Donald Wuerl of the Roman Catholic Diocese of Pittsburgh led the crowd in a pre-game prayer and then asked for a moment of silence. Members of the Air Force Reserve 911 Airlift Wing sang the national anthem and God Bless America. The players and fans sang along with them. Some wiped tears from their eyes. The fans placed $88,598 in collection baskets for disaster relief. Valentine and Pirates manager Lloyd McClendon hugged each other.

"I expected to see a tear, and I hope it doesn't end with one game," Valentine said. "But you can't tell how people will react."

For the Mets, helping the city and country heal was just beginning.

"It's hard, but we have a job to do," Franco said. "I don't know if it feels right, but we've got to get on with our lives. We're playing a game while people are being dug out and it's sad, but it's our job and we have to make the best of it."

Said Mets starting pitcher Al Leiter, a New Jersey native: "Over time, things will get better. It's the same when you lose a loved one. It's like anything in life. Time heals."

The Mets, wearing the special caps they had donned for the pregame ceremonies, played their first game back with can't-lose urgency. Leiter pitched seven strong innings and the score was tied, 1-1, in the top of the ninth inning when Rey Ordonez's RBI single and Mark Johnson's two-run double made a winner out of Franco, the only native New Yorker on the team. There were as many cheers and boos from the crowd when the go-ahead run scored. The win was the Mets' 18th in twenty-three games and moved them a game closer to Atlanta.

"For three hours, I hope we gave some pleasure to the guys who have been working," Franco said, referring to the rescue crews at the World Trade Center. "We're not playing just for ourselves, we're playing for the whole city of New York."

Said Johnson: "We wanted to win for the people of New York, play well and hopefully make some people back there feel better. It just seemed like the first four or five innings, the guys didn't know what to do. It was a weird feeling being back out there. Under the circumstances, it was tough. You could see it in Johnny's [Franco's] eyes, you can see how drained Al [Leiter] is. He pitched great and

Mets reliever John Franco—the only New York City native on the team—wears a Fire Department of New York cap in the dugout before the Mets resumed their season on September 17, six days after the terrorist attacks. The Mets wore hats from the fire department, the police department and EMS services in pre-game ceremonies to honor crews who worked the disaster in New York.

Johnny is so close to those guys, the rescue workers, you can see how much it meant to him."

The next night, Piazza hit a two-run homer in the eighth inning and the Mets won again, 7-5, to reach .500 for the first time since the opening week of the season. Already, there was a feeling that something special was happening, that the Mets were becoming America's Team and were prepared to pull off a miracle. The Mets were now only six games behind the Braves.

"We're playing good ball," Piazza said. "You don't know how far it's going to take us, but we just have to keep going."

Still wearing their special caps, the Mets completed a three-game sweep with a 9-2 victory on September 19. The Braves lost again, and the Mets were only five games back.

"Maybe we can do something in the last couple of weeks that will inspire people," first baseman Todd Zeile said.

As the Mets prepared to return to New York for what they knew would be an emotional three-game series—they just didn't know how emotional—against the Braves, the players, coaches, and Valentine announced that they would donate one day's pay to the fund established by former player Rusty Staub that benefits the widows and children of New York City policemen, firemen and emergency service workers killed in the line of duty: nearly $500,000. One day's pay for Piazza is $68,306. For Ventura, Kevin Appier and Leiter, $45,802, $43,716 and $40,984 respectively.

"It was time to put our money where our mouth is," Leiter said. "We're blessed to make a very good living. This is the least we can do."

"It's a sign that baseball players care," Valentine said. "Hopefully, it's an example, and others will follow their lead."

September 21, Shea Stadium: Baseball returns to New York for the first time since September 11. A crowd of 41,235 for a night that will never be forgotten in the storied history of New York baseball. Again, the teams lined up along the foul lines before the game for a tribute to the victims of the World Trade Center attack. The Mets wore their special caps and had 9-11-02 embroidered on their uniform sleeves. The ceremonies featured a color guard comprised of members of the New York City police and fire departments, emergency medical services and the Port Authority police. A large American flag was unfurled in the outfield, and a moment of silence was followed by a 21-gun salute honoring New Yorkers who died at the World Trade Center. New York City Mayor Rudy Guiliani, a Yankees fan who is normally booed at Shea, received a loud ovation, and Valentine led the crowd in a chant of, "Rudy! Rudy!" Diana Ross sang "God Bless America."

In a scene that might never be repeated, the arch-rival Mets and Braves hugged each other, and the crowd cheered both teams...even the hated Chipper Jones. After the first pitch, the ball was taken out of play and given to Giuliani.

"I'll give it to one of the children who has lost their father," the mayor said.

"The first couple of innings were tough," Jones said. "You can't go from the emotions at 7:15 and then put it right behind you. I have never been so jittery. In my first at-bat, I didn't have a chance."

During the seventh inning stretch, singer Liza Minelli offered a rousing rendition of "New York, New York," and the entire crowd sang along. She climbed on top of the dugout, punching out every word, and when she came to, "Come on come through, New York, New York," the crowd sang louder. Then, with the Mets trailing, 2-1, in the bottom of the eighth, Piazza launched a towering two-run homer to centerfield to win the game.

"I'm just so happy I gave the people something to cheer," Piazza said. "There was a lot of emotion. It was just a surreal sort of energy out there. I'm just so proud to be a part of it tonight. New York has been so strong through all this. I feel so sad. I met two kids today who lost their fathers. I'm glad to give people a diversion from the sorrow, to give them a thrill. If the season ends tomorrow, we're all winners, because we didn't give up. New York has been so strong throughout this. We just want to stay positive. This is what America is all about — coming together."

"I believe there are small miracles in every facet of life," Valentine said. "Maybe this was a small one tonight."

Said Zeile: "Baseball takes an absolute backseat tonight. People came to the park to unite. I think it starts to become about baseball tomorrow. But with us, it's intertwined, and it will be from now on."

The Mets were four and a half games out of first place. The next day, they beat the Braves again, 7-3, to move three and a half games out. They were 5-0 since play resumed and had gained four and a half games in six days. Steve Trachsel pitched seven strong innings and the Mets looked unstoppable.

"Yesterday was emotional and the crowd was great again tonight," Trachsel said. "It's still difficult to concentrate after what happened, but the support is great and if we can get this done, it would be special for the city."

But the magic hadn't touched everybody, most notably Mets closer Armando Benitez. The next afternoon, Leiter pitched eight strong innings and the Mets took a 4-1 lead into the ninth inning. The Braves were primed for a sweep. The Mets were about to move two and a half games back. The crowd was stomping its feet and cheering. A miracle was happening before their very eyes.

And then Benitez, who had failed so many times before in big games, failed again. He had two outs and two strikes on Brian Jordan, but Jordan kept the at-bat alive by fouling off several pitchers, then homered to left. The Mets still had a 4-3 lead, but Benitez took care of that in a hurry, and three batters later, B.J. Surhoff singled in the tying run. The crowd was stunned. Then, in the eleventh inning, Jordan homered again, this time off of Jerrod Riggan, to win the game. Once again, the Mets were four and a half games out of first, but now they had only twelve games remaining.

Benitez had single-handedly ended the miracle run.

The Mets refused to give up. Two nights later in Montreal, they beat the Expos, 2-0. A 5-2 win on Wednesday and a 12-6 win on Thursday made the Mets 8-1 since September 11 and gave them hope going into a pivotal three-game series against the Braves in Atlanta. The Mets were only three games out of first.

"I don't know if we ever like playing in Atlanta, but it sure is exciting," Valentine said. "For all that was said in May, June, July and August, that when we go there it wasn't going to mean anything, words don't mean anything. I like these guys when they're inspired, and they're inspired."

But Turner Field, which has always been the Mets' house of horrors, was no better to them this time. In the opener, Jones hit a two-run homer to break a tie and the Braves won, 5-3, to move four games ahead.

"It's a setback for us, but I'm optimistic," Piazza said. "If we can get even again tomorrow, by no means is it mathematically over."

The Mets looked as if they would get even. Again, Leiter pitched eight strong innings. This time, the Mets had a 5-1 lead going into the bottom of the ninth inning when Valentine handed Benitez the ball. And, once again, Benitez fell on his face and took the Mets with him.

Andruw Jones singled to lead off. With one out, Javy Lopez singled, scoring Jones. With two outs, pinch-hitter Keith Lockhart walked. Benitez looked rattled. Marcus Giles doubled to left, scoring Lopez and Lockhart, and making the score 5-4. Julio Franco was walked intentionally and Valentine replaced Benitez with Franco. Pinch-hitter Wes Helms loaded the bases, bringing up Jordan once again. One swing of the bat later, the Braves had an 8-5 lead. As the ball sailed into the seats, Franco put his hands on his hat and walked disgustedly toward the Mets' dugout before removing his hat and tossing it aside.

"We are playing not only or us, but for all the people we hope to bring some hope for," Franco said. "It's a tough one to swallow."

The 8-5 loss dropped the Mets five games behind the Braves with only seven games to play. For all intents and purposes, their season was over.

And so, they handed the job of making miracles to their crosstown rivals, the New York Yankees. The city still had one last chance for joy.

13

NEW YORK YANKEES
COME ON COME THROUGH, NEW YORK, NEW YORK

> *"If they win the World Series this year, we're going to remember it for the rest of our lives. They won the World Series the year we got bombed."*
> —LUIS VICENTE, 28, OF THE BRONX, TO THE *Bergen Record*

> *"It's up to you, New York, New York."*
> —FROM THE SONG "NEW YORK, NEW YORK," PLAYED AFTER EVERY YANKEES HOME WIN

WITH THE METS GONE, New York's hopes fell into the hands of the Yankees. Good hands, no doubt. The Yankees had won three straight World Series—four of the last five—and had won the American League East by 13½ over the Red Sox, winning every key game they played down the stretch. They were 6-0 against Boston, their nearest competitor, in August and September, and seemed to have retained that old Yankees magic, even though they were undoubtedly an aging team. After all, their best pitcher, Roger Clemens, was 39 years old, and one of their best players, Paul O'Neill, planned to retire after the playoffs.

But other teams looked like they might be better. The Mariners had won an American League record 116 games. And their first-round opponent, the Oakland A's, who finished second in the West, had won 102 games, seven more than the Yankees.

"These guys are good," Yankees relief pitcher Mike Stanton said of the Athletics. "You can talk about their age, but when it comes right down to it, these guys know how to play ball."

Said manager Joe Torre: "They are impressive. They were good last year, and they are better this year. And we held on by our teeth last year."

The Yankees had won the 2000 American League Division Series over Oakland, three games to two, and this year's test figured to be no easier.

The test looked tougher when the Yankees lost Game One, 5-3, to the A's at Yankee Stadium. Even more alarmingly, Clemens, who had gone 20-3 during the regular season, left in the fifth inning with a hamstring problem, and no one knew when he'd be able to pitch again. Clemens said he suffered the injury while going after a groundball to his right side in the fourth, but he hadn't seemed right all game.

"Sometimes you can look back to a certain at-bat and get upset," O'Neill said. "We just got flat out beat."

It was the third time in six years that the Yankees lost Game One of the first round. In 1996 against Texas and 2000 against Oakland, they won Game Two.

"It's something that you wish you never had to do," Stanton said. "If nothing else, we know that we can do it."

But they didn't do it. Andy Pettitte pitched well in Game Two, allowing only one run in six-plus innings, but the Yankees couldn't put anything on the board against A's righty Tim Hudson and lost, 2-0. Suddenly, after two straight losses at home, the Yankees were one loss away from being eliminated. All hopes of an October run to revitalize scarred, demoralized New York seemed lost.

"Right now, we have our backs against the wall with these guys," centerfielder Bernie Williams said. "It doesn't get any easier. We've got to put this one behind us, have a good workout tomorrow and let it all out on Saturday."

But the A's had won their last seventeen games at Network Associates Stadium in Oakland, and eight straight against the Yankees overall, including the regular season.

"I don't know about old, but they're certainly making us eat some dust right now," Torre said. "What we have to do is what we've done before, not necessarily in postseason: We have to go on a three-game winning streak."

The Yankees needed to win two games in Oakland just to force a deciding Game Five in New York, and their hopes looked dim as A's starter Barry Zito held them hitless through four innings. But Mike Mussina matched him pitch-for-pitch, and when catcher Jorge Posada homered in the fourth inning, the Yankees had all they needed for a 1-0 victory. Ace reliever Mariano Rivera pitched the last two innings for the save, and the Yankees were one game closer.

The Yankees had looked like the real Yankees—the Yankees capable of a dynasty—in Game Three. In the bottom of the sixth, third baseman Scott Brosius leaped to catch a line drive and second baseman Chuck Knoblauch made a super sliding catch on Jason Giambi's foul pop. Then, in the seventh inning, with the Yankees leading, 1-0, and Jeremy Giambi on first, shortstop Derek Jeter made one of the greatest plays in playoff history. With two outs, leftfielder Terrence Long lined a double into the rightfield corner. Giambi was waved home, and Shane Spencer's throw from rightfield soared past the cutoff men, late-inning replacement second baseman Alfonso Soriano and first baseman Tino Martinez. The ball bounced once, slowly, but by that time, Jeter had raced across the diamond from second base as the *secondary* backup. He nabbed it, then flipped it backhanded into catcher Posada's glove from ten feet away. Posada tagged Giambi for the third out.

"That's my job, and I did it," Jeter said. "I've made that play to second base before, but I'm the cutoff man. When I saw the third base coach motioning him around, I thought the throw wouldn't make it and that's when I stepped in. If we had lost the game, you guys [the media] probably couldn't have cared less about the play."

"I didn't know that he [Spencer] had missed the cutoff man," Giambi said. "I was picking up [third base coach Ron] Washington and coming in and getting ready to make some contact with Posada and I didn't see that he had the ball yet. So I figured that I had a better chance to try to run through the bag."

Torre insisted that the Yankees had worked on the play in spring training, but it was difficult to believe that what Jeter had done was part of their daily drills.

"Yeah, we worked on it, I think," Brosius said, "but it's still an incredible heads-up play. You don't practice the old run-towards-the-dugout-backhand-flip at home."

"What in the heck was Jeter doing there?" asked A's centerfielder Johnny Damon. "There's no way a shortstop would be there to back up. I saw him streaking across the field. The shovel pass was perfect. It saved the game for them."

"That's why he gets $18-million," Yankees infielder Luis Sojo said of Jeter. "He does everything."

Who knows what would have happened if Jeter hadn't made the play? The game would have been tied and the A's would've had the potential series-winning run on second. The Yankees had been doing nothing at the plate; they would finish with only two hits.

The Yankees would need more in Game Four. Starter Orlando Hernandez had an 8-1 record in the playoffs, but he had undergone toe surgery during the season and had experienced discomfort in his right elbow just a week ago. Yet, hours before Game Four, the Yankees sat in their clubhouse and acted as if they were the team in control of the series. They were relaxed, poised.

"We were just joking around," outfielder Bernie Williams said. "It seemed pretty relaxed. We were just watching a couple of the games on the East Coast and some of the football games. A lot of the guys were preparing. A lot of the guys were taking treatment. A lot of the guys were eating breakfast."

And then the Yankees went out and had the A's for lunch. They took advantage of an error to score two in the second. In the third,

Williams struck a two-run double to the deepest part of the park, scoring Jeter and David Justice. The A's responded with two in the bottom of the inning, but Williams drove in two more runs in the fourth to cap a three-run inning, and the Yankees were on their way to a 9-2 victory that, incredibly, silenced the crowd, left the A's stunned and sent the series back to New York for a decisive Game Five.

"We were all aware of the situation," Williams said. "There was no sense in rubbing it in. We knew we were down two games to one, and it was a must-win situation, but you don't want to be pins and needles out there."

"Surprised? I guess I can't be," Torre said. "We've done so many things the last six years that make me proud, and this certainly goes up there among the proudest."

The A's refused to concede that they were in trouble and that the Yankees were a steamroller that was about to run them over. "We're not shaken at all," A's manager Art Howe said. "I expected this to go five games. We were pretty fortunate to come in here two up. I wish I wasn't a soothsayer, but I thought it would go five. Hopefully, we can turn the tables on them tomorrow."

But anybody who had paid attention over the past four years knew the A's didn't stand a chance at Yankees Stadium in front of 56,642 fans who sensed that their team was on a magical run. No team had ever won the ALDS after losing the first two games at home, but the Yankees were unlike any other team.

"Just because it hasn't been done doesn't mean it can't be done," Stanton said. "That was our approach. If you look at the whole mountain, it looks impassable. But you start taking baby steps, and all of a sudden you're on top."

Emotion and hope was on the Yankees' side. Before the game, a policeman sang the national anthem and the crowd sang along. There were almost as many NYPD caps in the crowd as there were Yankees caps. The meaning of the game couldn't be ignored: after the tragedy of September 11, New York needed this one. A Yankees victory wouldn't bring back any lost lives, or lessen the tragedy, but it would give New York something to feel good about.

And the A's looked rattled. They made three errors. Their pitchers hit two batters. They scored off starter Roger Clemens in the first two innings to take a 2-0 lead. In the bottom of the second, Alfonso Soriano delivered a two-run single off starter Mark Mulder to tie the game, then took advantage of Oakland mistakes. In the third, catcher Greg Myers dropped a third strike, allowing Williams to reach first. Tino Martinez was hit by a pitch. Williams moved to third on a deep flyout to center, Shane Spencer walked to load the bases and Brosius hit a grounder to third for what should have been the third out. But Eric Chavez bobbled the ball, Williams scored and the Yankees had the lead for good. Rivera retired the A's in the last two innings and the Yankees made history with a 5-3 win. Again, Jeter made a spectacular play, and again he did it against Terrence Long, leaping into the stands along the thirdbase line to catch Long's foul popup in the eighth, sending the crowd into a frenzy.

"To come back like this against that ballclub, I mean, they are so good," Torre said. "It was very special."

"Everything that this city has gone through and the fans have gone through, just the opportunity to give them something to cheer about was a joy," Clemens said. "They were so loud."

When the game ended, Torre and New York City Mayor Rudy Giuliani walked off the field arm-in-arm as the crowd sang "New York, New York" along with Frank Sinatra.

"There was no question we knew there was a great deal of responsibility on our shoulders," Torre said. "We did have a piece in our heart of what went on and all the people that we take for granted."

In the clubhouse after their victory, the Yankees held a low-key celebration. They removed their caps and replaced them with those of the New York Police Department, Fire Department and Port Authority.

"To come back like this is perfect for the spirit of the city," Giuliani said.

Their next hurdle, the record-setting Mariners, seemed no less imposing, but the Yankees were ready.

"We're used to playing big games," O'Neill said. "We've got jitters and nerves like everybody else, but when we take the field, we've been successful."

So Pettitte pitched eight innings of three-hit ball and the sellout crowd at Safeco Field sat and watched as the Yankees scored a workmanlike 4-2 victory in Game One. Two cross-country trips in one week seemed to have no effect on the Yankees, who were riding on emotion. In Game Two at Safeco, the Yankees scored three runs

(Opposite page) Mariano Rivera, the best closer in baseball, had two saves for the Yankees in the American League Division Series against the A's and two more in the American League Championship Series against the Mariners. The Yankees came from two games down to beat the A's in five, then eliminated the Mariners, four games to one.

in the second on a two-run double by Brosius and an RBI single by Knoblauch, and although the Mariners scored two in the fourth off Mussina to cut New York's lead to 3-2, they might as well have been a hundred runs behind. Ramiro Mendoza and Rivera closed down the Mariners in the last three innings, and the Yankees went home with a two games to none lead.

The Mariners? Their 116 regular-season wins suddenly seemed like a mirage.

"We're going to be back here to play Game Six, OK?" Mariners manager Lou Piniella said, not really sounding like he believed his own words. "I've got confidence in my baseball club. We've gone to New York and beat this baseball team five out of six times, and we're going to do it again."

For one night, Piniella looked like he might be right. The Mariners scored seven runs in the sixth inning of Game Three and won, 14-3, at Yankee Stadium. The fourteen runs set an American League Championship Series record. Was it possible that the Yankees, after coming back from losing the first two games in the Division Series, would now lose the ALCS after winning the first two games in Seattle?

Game Four was a battle. Starters Paul Abbott and Clemens battled through five scoreless innings. The bullpens took over, and the game was still scoreless when the Mariners batted in the eighth. Bret Boone hit a solo homer off of Mendoza to give Seattle a 1-0 lead, and suddenly the Yankees were in trouble. But Williams homered to right with one out in the bottom of the inning to tie the game, Rivera retired the Mariners in order in the ninth, and with one out in the Yankees half, Brosius reached on an infield single off reliever Kaz Sasaki, bringing up rookie Alfonso Soriano. With the count one-oh, Sasaki threw a fastball over the middle of the plate. Soriano swung.

"I just concentrated on connecting well with the ball and going after it," the 23-year-old Soriano said.

The crowd stood and watched. Soriano stood and watched. The ball sailed toward rightfield. Outfielder Mike Cameron went back to the fence and jumped, but the ball, helped by a stiff wind, sailed over the fence, giving the Yankees a 3-1 victory and igniting a wild celebration on the field and in the stands.

"We just jumped off the bench," Tino Martinez said. "We knew it was gone when he hit it."

"For a minute, I thought I had a play on it," Cameron said. "But it didn't seem like it wanted to be played."

"I think we're just blessed," Williams said. "It has taken a lot of work. It has a lot to do with the attitude of this club."

"I don't know if you can get any higher than this," Torre said. "We're going to have to calm down for a game tomorrow."

But the Mariners had no life left. Pettitte pitched six strong innings. Williams homered. O'Neill homered. The Yankees led, 9-0, after six innings, and the delirious crowd spent the rest of the game singing and celebrating. The Yankees won, 12-3, to end the Mariners' season and reach their fourth straight World Series. On October 22, the Yankees' magical, heroic run had reached its climax.

Down 0-2 to Oakland, they won.

Facing the best team in baseball, they won.

Playing for a city that needed something to cheer about, they won.

"This ballclub will be remembered by me forever," Torre said. "A lot of what went on in this city, and down 0-2 to Oakland, makes this special. Down 2-0 to one of the best clubs in baseball, you never, never, never doubted yourselves. This city needed something like this. We needed something like this."

Major League Commissioner Bud Selig had asked teams not to pop champagne after post-season victories out of respect to those who died on September 11, but Torre defied the order in classy fashion. After the game, he offered a simple champagne toast to his team and to those who had died. The Yankees were the toast of baseball.

"To get to this point is very gratifying," Tino Martinez said. "I like to think it's destiny. The city's gone through a lot, the country's gone through a lot, but mainly the city. We try to represent New York City well."

The Yankees, who have always been the most-beloved and most-hated team in baseball, suddenly were gaining new fans who wanted them to win just for the sake of New York. Even Mariners manager Lou Piniella found reason for happiness in the Yankees' win.

"The amazing thing is that in the eighth inning," Piniella said, "when the fans were really reveling in the stands, the one thought that did come to my mind strangely enough is, 'Boy, this city has suffered a lot and tonight they let out a lot of emotions.' I felt good for them in a way, not that we were getting beat or not that we were getting beat up, but I felt good for them. I really did."

Said Mussina: "I know the last two innings of Game Four and the entire Game Five were a pretty exciting eleven innings of baseball at the Stadium. I know players that have been here for a few years, Hall of Famers, people that have come in the clubhouse, have said it was the loudest they've ever witnessed the Stadium. I know there are a lot of New Yorkers letting out a lot of energy. It's fun to see, it's great to see."

"When you realize what we have done here, before the tragedy of September 11, we turned New York, eight or nine million people, into a small town," Torre said. "When you go through the Canyon of Heroes and you see those people hanging out of windows and on light posts and the looks on their faces, squeezed up against one another, you realize how special it is to have a city the size of New York come together. Then you have the terrible tragedy on the 11th. To see them come together again, for obviously a different reason, for compassion and love and strength, you realize this is a very special team. And I'm proud of my team, the way they've come together to really maybe help the city through tough times, and even though there's a lot of tough times ahead, to give them something to root for, pull for and feel good about."

In the clubhouse after the game, Giuliani said, "There's no question the city needs a lift and the Yankees delivered a tremendous lift when they beat Oakland and this is even greater. Baseball can help tremendously. If you've traveled around the city in the last week to ten days, everybody has become Yankee fans. I think their comeback victory against Oakland really is the thing that did it. This can have a tremendous impact on the spirit of the city, and it has already."

"I think we've lifted spirits," Pettitte said. "There's a lot of stuff going on right now, around the world and obviously here, that's very bad. People are scared and nervous about things, and yet we're still able to put 60,000 people in the Stadium and they can come and cheer for us like they never cheered before. That's special. It gives them a chance to put some things off their minds. We've been a great story and that makes it even better for them. We've shown a lot of heart and the city has shown a lot of heart. I think we're kind of feeding off everything that's going on."

The Yankees' victory didn't lessen the suffering, but it seemed to symbolize New York's resolve in the face of tragedy. And now, as they headed into the World Series, the Yankees were truly America's Team.

THE WORLD SERIES

14

THE GREATEST WORLD SERIES EVER

WHY SHOULDN'T IT HAVE ENDED THIS WAY? The greatest season in baseball history was worthy of a remarkable conclusion. Otherwise, it would be like having the cake without the icing, the party without the guest of honor.

But who could have expected anything so special? The Yankees, afterall, had won twenty-six World Series and four of the last five, including three straight. They had already made an improbable comeback to escape defeat in the first round of the playoffs, and had made the powerful Seattle Mariners look like just another team in the American League Championship Series.

The Diamondbacks? What had they ever done? They were in only their fourth season. They had never played in the World Series and seemed to be a two-gun team: ace pitchers Randy Johnson and Curt Schilling.

This one looked like a mismatch. History was on the Yankees' side. Everything was on the Yankees' side. Next victim: the Arizona Diamondbacks.

But then we settled down for seven games of unforgettable drama.

In Game One, the Diamondbacks looked nothing like a team making its World Series debut, while the Yankees looked nothing like a team that had won three straight championships. Schilling was outstanding and the D-Backs won, 9-1, at Bank One Ballpark in Phoenix, thanks to five unearned runs, the most in a Series game since 1973.

"Just getting a win in Game One was huge," Arizona manager Bob Brenly said. "But I don't think there is any carryover effect from the score."

Craig Counsell, the Marlins' hero in the 1997 World Series, homered and so did Luis Gonzalez as Yankees pitcher Mike Mussina struggled throughout. When Mark Grace doubled home two runs in the fourth inning to make it 9-1, the crowd settled in for a rout.

The victory was key for the Diamondbacks, who realized their best chance to win the series was to have Schilling and Johnson win their games, and for the aces to pitch as many games as possible. Schilling pitched seven innings, allowing three hits and struckout eight. Afterward, he had an ominous message for the Yanks.

"I feel real good," he said after throwing only 102 pitches. "I didn't throw a lot of pitches tonight. If I have to come back on three days' rest, I'll be ready."

The Yankees hadn't been held to three or fewer hits in a World Series game since 1963.

"I know all about the history of the Yankees," Schilling said. "But I wasn't pitching against Babe Ruth or Mickey Mantle today. I was pitching against these Yankees."

And these Yankees weren't looking too good. David Justice dropped a fly ball in the third, leading to two unearned runs. Scott Brosius also bobbled a grounder in the fourth, leading to more runs. But the Diamondbacks, knowing the Yankees' history of coming back, refused to gloat over the rout.

"Knowing them, all we did tonight was probably wake them up," Grace said. "I don't think we sent them a message. These guys have returned many messages over the years."

The Diamondbacks were in such a precarious position with the rest of their pitching staff that a victory in Game Two with Johnson on the mound was as important for them as it was for the Yankees, who with a victory would have the chance to return home and win three straight games and the Series. Andy Pettitte was on the mound for the Yankees, and his post-season record made him an imposing opponent for the D-Backs.

But Johnson, making his first World Series start, out-dueled Pettitte through the first six innings before the Diamondbacks broke through on Matt Williams's three-run homer in the seventh off Pettitte for a 4-0 lead. That turned out to be the final score, as The Big Unit pitched a complete game three-hitter, striking out 11 and, more importantly, throwing only 110 pitches, keeping him fresh.

"I got to enjoy the game last night, watching Curt pitch," Johnson said. "It was nice, obviously, to take two ballgames, but this is far from over."

"This was one of those games where we were just dominated," Yankees shortstop Derek Jeter said, referring to Johnson's performance. "They're not just pitching well against me. They were pitching well against everyone."

"He was terrific," Yankees manager Joe Torre said. "He lived up to what he's supposed to be. The axiom has never changed: good pitching stops good hitting. And that's what we've seen."

The Yankees had their last chance in the top of the eighth inning. Shane Spencer and Alfonso Soriano started the inning with singles, but Johnson got Brosius looking at a 97-mile-per-hour fastball, then got pinch-hitter Luis Sojo to ground into a double-play.

"We've never been a ballclub that planned to go out and outscore somebody," Torre said. "We need to pitch. We need to dominate. Andy Pettitte was terrific, but Randy Johnson was better. So certainly we need the Rocket to set the tone."

"All we've done is win two games," Grace said. "We did what we had to do, win the first two games with our big boys. They're still standing and we know what they did against the Braves." He was referring to the Yankees' comeback win in the 1996 World Series, when they lost the first two games against the Braves and won the next four.

The Yankees knew they had the advantage in Game Three. Cold,

Mr. November: Derek Jeter of the Yankees hits the game-winning homerun in the tenth inning of Game Four, tying the series at two games each. The clock had just struck midnight, marking the first time a World Series game was played in November.

windy Yankee Stadium. Roger Clemens vs. Brian Anderson. History. But there was nothing easy about this game for the sudden underdogs.

It was another emotional night at Yankee Stadium. President George Bush was on hand to throw out the first pitch, and he threw a perfect strike that, to many people, symbolized American resolve after the September 11 terrorist attacks. Straight down the middle. Then Clemens took the mound and started throwing unhittable heat down the middle. The Diamondbacks couldn't touch him.

But the Yankees weren't exactly doing great things against seemingly overmatched Brian Anderson. A leadoff homerun in the second inning by Jorge Posada was matched by Matt Williams's one-out sacrifice fly in the top of the fourth, plating Chuck Finley. Neither team was mounting much offense until the bottom of the sixth, when Bernie Williams led off with a single. With one out, Williams moved to second on a wild pitch by Anderson, then Posada walked. Anderson, who had already thrown 107 pitches, was relieved by Mike Morgan, who struckout David Justice for the second out. But, with the crowd standing, Brosius hit a broken-bat single to left, scoring Williams with the go-ahead run.

Then the game was in the hands of the Yankees pitchers. Clemens, who allowed only three hits, pitched two more scoreless innings and closer Mariano Rivera retired all six batters he faced—including four consecutive strikeouts—to wrap up the 2-1 victory that cut Arizona's series lead in half.

"I knew it was a game that we had to have," Clemens said. "It was exciting to be part of everything. It was something I'll always have with me."

The Diamondbacks, hardly looking like the team that had dominated in Arizona, made three errors. "It's tough to come here," Anderson said. "We knew it was going to be tough trying to beat them on their home field."

Although his team still had the lead, D-Backs manager Bob Brenly was clearly feeling the pressure. After the game, he announced that Schilling would start Game Four on only three days rest.

"He's the right guy," Brenly said. "He said all along he's prepared to pitch. I mean, he didn't do cartwheels or anything like that when I told him and he didn't look at me like I was crazy."

Asked about his history of pitching on three days' rest, Schilling said, "Don't have one. Never done it before in the big leagues."

The time had come for the 2001 World Series to turn into a classic.

Game Four. Schilling vs. Orlando "El Duque" Hernandez. The Diamondbacks threatened in the first three innings, but couldn't score. In the bottom of the third, Shane Spencer led off with a homer against Schilling to give the Yankees a 1-0 lead. That was all they would get off the Mariners' ace, who looked as good on three days rest as he had in Game One. In the top of the fourth, Hernandez seemed to have escaped trouble when, after allowing a leadoff single, he enduced a double-play ball. But Grace homered to rightfield to tie the game.

Schilling started to dominate. He retired the Yankees in order in the fourth and fifth innings. Brosius hit a leadoff double to faraway center in the sixth, but Soriano couldn't move him over, and Schilling got Jeter and O'Neill on grounders to end the inning. In the top of the seventh, Grace walked with one out and moved to second when Hernandez clunked Damian Miller with a pitch. Mike Stanton relieved Hernandez, who had allowed only four hits in six-and-one-third innings, and ended the threat when Mark Womack hit into a double play.

The Yankees threatened in the bottom of the seventh. Williams singled to left. Tino Martinez walked, and New York had the go-ahead run on second. Was Schilling tiring? No, as it turned out. He got Jorge Posada to ground into a doubleplay, then, with Williams on third, fanned Justice swinging.

But the Diamondbacks needed to score before the Yankees did, otherwise they'd again face the daunting task of trying to rally against Rivera. With one out in the eighth, Gonzalez singled to center. Then little-known replacement Erubiel Durazo (he had batted only 175 times during the season) doubled to deep center, scoring Gonzalez with the go-ahead run. The Diamondbacks made it 3-1 one batter later, then put the game into the hands of closer Byung Hyun Kim, a 22-year-old from South Korea who had saved 19 games during the season.

Kim dominated the Yanks in the bottom of the eighth, striking out Spencer, Brosius and Soriano. When Jeter grounded out to lead off the bottom of the ninth, the Yankees were two outs away from facing a daunting task: down three games to one with Johnson and Schilling pitching two of the final three games, two of which would be played in Arizona. O'Neill singled to keep the Yankees' hopes alive, but Kim struck out Bernie Williams.

Over in the visitor's dugout, the Diamondbacks were ready for a celebration. In the home dugout, the Yankees looked glum. The crowd was quiet. Tino Martinez, who had been hitless in nine World Series at-bats, stepped to the plate. Kim threw. Martinez swung and made contact. The ball soared into the night air toward centerfield. Would it have enough to leave the ballpark? It did, and, incredibly, the game was tied. The crowd roared. The Yankees celebrated. But they had only tied the game, not won it.

Rivera retired the Diamondbacks in the tenth. Kim started the tenth, his third inning of work, and retired Brosius and Soriano. Jeter came up. The clock struck twelve. The scoreboard read, "Welcome to November Baseball." And Jeter tried to become the first Mr. November.

Kim had two strikes on Jeter, who had been only one-for-15 in the series. Jeter fouled off the next three pitches. Kim wound up and fired his 61st pitch, a big number for a short reliever. Jeter swung and sent the ball on a line toward the rightfield seats. Everything that happened next seemed to happen in slow motion: Jeter watching the ball, the crowd rising and watching with him, Kim turning in disbelief. The ball landing in the rightfield seats as the scoreboard clock showed 12:04. The game was over. The series was tied.

"We always feel as though we have a chance to win a game," Jeter said. "When you get to the postseason, you can throw everything out that you've done in the regular season. We never gave up. No matter what the score is, we feel like we can come back."

"Surprising things happen," Torre said. "Yet, when you think about it, it doesn't surprise you, because this ballclub never quits."

It was the first time in World Series history that a team had tied the game on a homer in the ninth and won it with a homer in extra innings.

"We had a lead, we had six outs left to go in the ballgame," Brenly said. "That's the way we hoped it would work out. Unfortunately, it didn't."

The series was going back to Arizona, but first, Mussina, the Game One loser, would square off against Miguel Batista (11-8 during the season) in Game Five. It couldn't be any better than Game Four . . . but it was.

The Yankees had as much trouble with Batista as they had with Schilling and Johnson. They went down meekly on only two hits in the first four innings before Arizona went to its power arsenal in the fifth. Finley homered to right to leadoff the inning, then with two outs, catcher Rod Barajas, a backup who had hit only .160 during the season and hadn't homered since April 21, deposited a

(Opposite page) Diamondbacks reliever Byung Hyun Kim is comforted by catcher Rod Barajas after giving up a game-tying, two-run homer to Scott Brosius of the Yankees in the ninth inning of Game Five. The Yankees went on to win the game, 3-2, in twelve innings, and take a three games to two lead. Kim blew two ninth-inning leads in two nights.

Mussina pitch into the leftfield seats. The Diamondbacks were up by two again.

Batista worked out of minor trouble in the fifth, then faced only three batters to retire the Yankees in the sixth. He got the first two batters in the seventh, walked Spencer, then retired Brosius on a flyball to right. The Yankees were in a familiar position: six outs to go, down by two.

The Diamondbacks threatened but didn't score in the eighth. In the home half, Batista retired the first two Yankees then walked O'Neill. Williams singled to center, O'Neill moved to third, and Brenly decided he had seen enough of Batista, who had thrown 126 pitches. Greg Swindell came on and got Martinez to fly out to left. The Diamondbacks were again three outs away from winning their third game.

Could it happen again? Was it possible? How much magic were the Yankees capable of?

Ramiro Mendoza retired the D-Backs in the ninth, and before the bottom of the ninth, many people were amazed to see Kim running in from the bullpen. He had thrown 61 pitches the night before and allowed two dramatic homeruns. Wasn't Brenly playing with fire?

"He's our closer," Brenly said. "He wanted the ball in that situation."

The sellout crowd roared and started taunting Kim. Posada led off the inning with a double, and Kim looked rattled. But he got Spencer on a groundout for the first out and struck out Knoblauch. For the second night in a row, he was one out away from victory.

Brosius walked to the plate. He took a step toward Kim and held up a finger, indicating, "One more out." He was challenging Kim to come up with the big out. But Kim couldn't get it. Brosius swung and made direct contact, launching a drive to leftfield that quickly left the ballpark. Again, the game was tied. Brosius raised his arm as he rounded the bases. Kim crouched on the mound. Brenly was motionless in the dugout.

"You know they have to be thinking, 'I can't believe this is happening.' Not one night, but two nights in a row," Mussina said.

146 | ONE FOR THE AGES: THE WORLD SERIES

Now a Yankees victory seemed inevitable, but the Diamondbacks refused to go quietly. In the eleventh, the Diamondbacks got their first two men on, then loaded the bases with one out against Rivera. With the Yankees playing back for the double-play, Reggie Sanders lined the ball up the middle, and Soriano made a diving catch for the second out. Then Rivera got Grace on a grounder to third to end the inning.

The Yankees went down in order in the eleventh. The Diamondbacks went quietly in the top of the twelfth. Albie Lopez relieved Mike Morgan for Arizona, and Knoblauch led off the Yankees twelfth with a single to center. Brosius sacrificed him to second. Soriano drove the ball into rightfield. It landed in front of Sanders. Knoblauch was waved home. Sanders had a chance to get him, but his one-hop throw eluded catcher Rod Barajas. Knoblauch slid under the phantom tag, and the Yankees had won the game, 3-2. Now they were the ones with the three games to two lead.

"This is the most incredible couple of games I've ever managed," Torre said. "This is *Groundhog Day*. I don't know what's going on. But I can't be surprised. It just happened the day before."

"No disrespect to the fans or the Diamondbacks, but you have to sit back and kind of chuckle a little bit because it's so unbelievable," Knoblauch said.

"You can't win them all. We would like to win them all, but the Yankees are very tough here in their house, and we know that," Brenly said.

Yankees magic seemed to have taken over. They had scored two of the most improbable victories in World Series history. Twice, they had rallied from two runs down in the ninth inning. Twice, they had won in extra innings. Even Randy Johnson and the imposing Bank One Ballpark crowd they'd face in Game Six didn't seem imposing. They had overcome so much already.

"We left New York scratching our heads," Luis Gonzalez said. "We had those games won."

But the Yankees weren't prepared for what they faced. In Game Six, the Diamondbacks set a World Series record with 22 hits and pounded the Yankees and Pettitte, 15-2. They scored eight runs in the third and had a 15-0 lead after four innings, enabling Brenly to pull Johnson whenever he wanted. Inexplicably, he waited until after the seventh. The crowd was in a merry mood. It serenaded the Yankees with Frank Sinatra's "New York, New York," and looked forward to Game Seven, when Schilling would have the chance to pitch again.

"I could not have come up with this: Game Seven vs. Roger Clemens," Schilling said. "I couldn't have dreamt this. I'm not that big a dreamer."

"It's a great setup," Tino Martinez said. "We've got our work cut out for us. They've got their work cut out for them. Winner take all. It's going to be exciting."

"I guess it is supposed to come down to seven," Torre said. "Roger against Curt. They are both 20-game winners. They are both in line for the Cy Young. You know, I think the fans will get a treat."

One beyond their wildest imaginations.

The pitching duel was one for the ages: Clemens and Schilling, two aces, both with their best stuff. Schilling coasted through the first two innings. In the bottom of the second, the Diamondbacks put two on with one out, but Clemens struckout the next two batters. Schilling again retired the side in order in the third. The D-Backs had two on with two out in the third, but Clemens got Finley swinging at the third strike. The Yankees went one-two-three in the fourth. Clemens struckout two more in the fourth. The game was looking like it might come down to who scored first.

The pitchers breezed through the fifth inning. Schilling seemed to be getting stronger. He K'd Soriano and Brosius to start the sixth and erased Clemens on a flyball to right. Through six innings, he had allowed only one hitter to reach base. The D-Backs finally broke through in the bottom of the sixth. Finley singled to center. Danny Bautista figured to bunt, but Brenly let him swing away and he drove a double into the gap in left-centerfield, scoring Finley. The 1-0 lead looked huge.

But Schilling gave it right back. He had retired sixteen straight batter before Jeter led off the seventh with a single. O'Neill singled to short center, and Schilling was in trouble for the first time all

night. Williams grounded out, moving Jeter to third, and Martinez tied the game with a single to right.

Mike Stanton relieved Clemens with one out in the seventh and got out of minor trouble. Alfonso Soriano homered to left off Schilling leading off the eighth, and now the Yankees' 2-1 lead looked insurmountable. With one out, Justice singled to center, and Brenly replaced Schilling with Miguel Batista. One out later, Brenly signalled to the bullpen for the man who had pitched seven innings the night before: Randy Johnson.

The Big Unit retired the side, but the Diamondbacks went meekly in the eighth against Mariano Rivera. They were in a position so many teams had failed in before: trying to rally in the late innings against the best closer in baseball. The Yankees had far more experience than the Diamondbacks, and Mariano Rivera was no Byung Hyun Kim.

Johnson gave his team a chance by retiring the Yankees in order in the ninth, and walked off the mound to a standing ovation. But the Yankees were three outs away from their fourth consecutive World Series.

Grace led off with a single. David Dellucci pinch-ran for Grace. Damian Miller came up in a bunting situation and bunted the ball toward Rivera. The pitcher fielded the ball cleanly, but threw the ball wide of second. The Diamondbacks had two on with none out. The next batter, Jay Bell, bunted into a force play at third. Now there were men on first and second with one out. Midre Cummings ran for Miller. Rivera had been in this situation before, and had almost always come through.

Womack belted a double into the rightfield corner, scoring Cummings with the tying run and sending Bell to third. Counsell, who scored the game-winning run in Game Seven of the 1997 World Series, was hit by a pitch to load the bases. Rivera suddenly looked mortal. And Luis Gonzalez, who was hitless in four at-bats for the night, stepped to the plate.

The infield moved in. Gonzalez, choking up on the bat for the first time all season, made contact and blooped a soft liner into centerfield. Williams raced in, but there was no way he could get to

(Opposite page) The final blow: Luis Gonzalez of the Diamondbacks bloops a single to knock in the World Series-winning run in the bottom of the ninth inning of Game Seven.

(Opposite page) The Diamondbacks can't believe it themselves. They celebrate after winning the World Series with a 3-2 victory over the Yankees in Game Seven.

it. Bell scored. The Diamondbacks were World Champions, and they had done it in only their fourth year of existence, breaking the record for fastest expansion team to win the Series set by the Marlins in 1997.

"When you're a little kid, you think about the seventh game of the World Series," Gonzalez said. "It didn't matter how the hit came. That was the one guy we wanted to stay away from the whole World Series. We got him the one time it counted."

"That's baseball," said Rivera, who had saved 23 straight post-season games. "There's nothing I can do about it."

Fireworks exploded. The crowd celebrated the first major league sports championship in Arizona history. The on-field celebration lasted over an hour. Johnson, the first pitcher to win three times in a World Series since Mickey Lolich in 1968, was named co-MVP along with Schilling.

"We went through sports' greatest dynasty to win our first World Series," Schilling said. "This is one of those things that is going to take a whole bunch of time to absorb."

Brenly became the first manager to win the World Series in his first year since 1961. And both teams left fans with lasting memories.

"That was the greatest Game Seven ever," New York City Mayor Rudy Giuliani said. "As a Yankees fan, I wish it turned out differently."

"We realize how many times we snatched it away from people when they were close, so you really have to take both sides of this thing," Torre said. "I certainly am proud of the way my ballclub responded to the pressure."

"Mark my words, this is going to go down as one of the greatest World Series ever played, from start to finish," Gonzalez said.

Said Yankees owner George Steinbrenner, who's never been a good loser, "This was a great World Series. Great for baseball."

It was the only way to complete the greatest season ever.

THE DIAMONDBACKS' ROAD TO THE WORLD SERIES

March 9, 1995: The Arizona Diamondbacks are born in Palm Beach, Florida, as Major League Baseball owners name the D-Backs and Tampa Bay Devil Rays the 13th and 14th expansion teams in history. Both teams will start play in the 1997 season.

November 13, 1995: Two seasons before their first opening day, the D-Backs name Buck Showalter as their manager.

November 27, 1997: Jay Bell leaves the Kansas City Royals to sign with the Diamondbacks and becomes the franchise's first major leaguer.

November 18, 1997: The Diamondbacks select 35 players in the expansion draft in Phoenix. Arizona's first choice is pitcher Brian Anderson of the Cleveland Indians.

December 1, 1997: Third baseman Matt Williams is acquired from the Cleveland Indians in a trade and signs a five-year contract extension.

February 13, 1998: Pitchers and catchers open the team's first spring training in Tucson, Arizona.

February 27, 1998: In the Diamondbacks' first Cactus League exhibition game, Edwin Diaz hits a ninth-inning sacrifice fly that scores Kelly Stinnett with the winning run in a 6-5 victory over the Chicago White Sox.

March 31, 1998: A sellout crowd of 50,179 at Bank One Ballpark watches the Diamondbacks lose their first game, 9-2, to the Colorado Rockies. Travis Lee gets the franchise's first hit, a single in the first inning. He also gets its first homer, run scored and RBI.

April 4, 1998: The Diamondbacks record their first win, 3-2 over San Francisco.

December 1, 1998: The Diamondbacks take their first major step toward winning the World Series by signing left-handed pitcher Randy Johnson, a Cy Young Award winner, from the Seattle Mariners.

February 26, 1999: The D-Backs acquire Tony Womack.

July 13, 1999: Williams and Bell become the first Diamondbacks to start an All-Star Game. Johnson and leftfielder Luis Gonzalez also appear in the game. The Diamondbacks have more players on the National League squad than any other team.

September 24, 1999: Matt Williams scoops up Doug Mirabelli's ground ball and throws to first base for the final out of an 11-3 victory in San Francisco that mathematically clinches the National League West championship for the Diamondbacks. Arizona becomes the first expansion team to reach the playoffs or win a division title in its second year of competition.

October 3, 1999: In their season finale, the Diamondbacks win their 100th game.

October 5, 1999: In the Diamondbacks' first post-season game, they lose to the Mets, 8-4, on a grand slam by Edgardo Alfonzo in the ninth inning.

October 6, 1999: Todd Stottlemyre allows four hits over six-plus innings as the Diamondbacks record their first playoff win, 7-1, over the Mets. Steve Finley's two-run single in the third puts Arizona ahead to stay.

October 9, 1999: The Diamondbacks lose to the New York Mets, 4-3, in the Division Series when Todd Pratt of the Mets homers in the bottom of the tenth inning.

November 16, 1999: Randy Johnson wins his second Cy Young Award and first by a Diamondbacks pitcher. He led the Major Leagues in strikeouts, innings pitched and complete games.

July 11, 2000: Johnson and outfielder Steve Finley represent the Diamondbacks in the All-Star Game. Johnson is the starting pitcher. Finley gets a single and an RBI.

July 26, 2000: The Diamondbacks acquire righthanded pitcher Curt Schilling from the Philadelphia Phillies for pitchers Omar Daal, Nelson Figueroa and Vicent Padilla and first baseman Travis Lee.

September 10, 2000: Johnson becomes the twelfth pitcher in Major League history to have 3,000 career strikeouts. He K's Mike Lowell of the Florida Marlins. He also records his 300th strikeout of the season, joining Nolan Ryan as the only pitchers to have 300 strikeouts in three consecutive seasons.

October 2, 2000: The Diamondbacks miss the playoffs and manager Buck Showalter is fired.

October 30, 2000: Broadcaster Bob Brenly is named the Diamondbacks' new manager.

November 14, 2000: Johnson wins his third Cy Young Award.

December 8, 2000: First baseman Mark Grace signs a two-year contract with the Diamondbacks.

April 26, 2001: Luis Gonzalez hits his 13th homer of the month, tying Ken Griffey Jr. for the most homeruns ever hit in April.

May 8, 2001: Johnson strikes out 20 Reds in nine innings. The Diamondbacks win in extra innings, 4-3.

August 29, 2001: Gonzalez hits his 50th homerun of the season.

October 5, 2001: The Diamondbacks clinch the National League West with a 5-0 win over the Milwaukee Brewers.

October 14, 2001: The Diamondbacks beat the Cardinals in Game Five to win the National League Division Series. It's the first post-season series win in franchise history.

October 21, 2001: The Diamondbacks beat the Braves, four games to one, to win the National League Championship Series. Craig Counsell is NLCS MVP.

November 4, 2001: In the bottom of the ninth inning of Game Seven of the World Series, Gonzalez singles home Jay Bell with the winning run as the Diamondbacks beat the Yankees, four games to three, for their first World Championship and Arizona's first major professional sports championship. The Diamondbacks needed only four seasons to win it all, a Major League record for expansion teams.

BONDS BEATS McGWIRE

Here's a list of the homeruns hit by Barry Bonds of the San Francisco Giants during the 2001 season, with the date, opposing team, opposing pitcher and number of men on base when he hit the homer.

1. April 2 .... vs. San Diego (Williams) 0
2. April 12 .... at San Diego (Eaton) 0
3. April 13 .... at Milwaukee (Wright) 1
4. April 14 .... at Milwaukee (Haynes) 2
5. April 15 .... at Milwaukee (Weathers) 0
6. April 17 .... vs. Los Angeles (Adams) 1
7. April 18 .... vs. Los Angeles (Park) 0
8. April 20 .... vs. Milwaukee (Haynes) 1
9. April 24 .... vs. Cincinnati (Brower) 1
10. April 26 .... vs. Cincinnati (Sullivan) 1
11. April 29 .... vs. Chicago Cubs (Aybar) 0
12. May 2 .... at Pittsburgh (Ritchie) 1
13. May 3 .... at Pittsburgh (Anderson) 1
14. May 4 .... at Philadelphia (Chen) 1
15. May 11 .... vs. New York Mets (Trachsel) 0
16. May 17 .... at Florida (Smith) 1
17. May 18 .... at Atlanta (Remlinger) 0
18. May 19 .... at Atlanta (Perez) 0
19. May 19 .... at Atlanta (Cabrera) 0
20. May 19 .... at Atlanta (Marquis) 0
21. May 20 .... at Atlanta (Burkett) 0
22. May 20 .... at Atlanta (Remlinger) 0
23. May 21 .... at Arizona (Schilling) 0
24. May 22 .... at Arizona (Springer) 1
25. May 24 .... vs. Colorado (Thomson) 0
26. May 27 .... vs. Colorado (Neagle) 1
27. May 30 .... vs. Arizona (Ellis) 0

28.	May 30	vs. Arizona (Ellis)	1
29.	June 1	at Colorado (Chacon)	1
30.	June 4	vs. San Diego (Jones)	0
31.	June 5	vs. San Diego (Serrano)	1
32.	June 7	vs. San Diego (Lawrence)	1
33.	June 12	vs. Anaheim (Rapp)	0
34.	June 14	vs. Anaheim (Pote)	0
35.	June 15	vs. Oakland (Mulder)	0
36.	June 15	vs. Oakland (Mulder)	0
37.	June 19	at San Diego (Eaton)	0
38.	June 20	at San Diego (Myers)	1
39.	June 23	at St. Louis (Kile)	1
40.	July 12	at Seattle (Abbott)	0
41.	July 18	vs. Colorado (Hampton)	0
42.	July 18	vs. Colorado (Hampton)	1
43.	July 26	at Arizona (Schilling)	0
44.	July 26	at Arizona (Schilling)	3
45.	July 27	at Arizona (Anderson)	0
46.	August 1	vs. Pittsburgh (Beimel)	0
47.	August 4	vs. Philadelphia (Figueroa)	1
48.	August 7	at Cincinnati (Graves)	0
49.	August 9	at Cincinnati (Winchester)	0
50.	August 11	at Chicago Cubs (Borowski)	2
51.	August 14	vs. Florida (Bones)	3
52.	August 16	vs. Florida (Burnett)	0
53.	August 16	vs. Florida (Darensbourg)	2
54.	August 18	vs. Atlanta (Marquis)	0
55.	August 23	at Montreal (Lloyd)	0
56.	August 27	at New York Mets (Appier)	0
57.	August 31	vs. Colorado (Thomson)	1
58.	September 3	vs. Colorado (Jennings)	0
59.	September 4	vs. Arizona (Batista)	0
60.	September 6	vs. Arizona (Lopez)	0
61.	September 9	at Colorado (Elarton)	0
62.	September 9	at Colorado (Elarton)	0
63.	September 9	at Colorado (Belitz)	2
64.	September 20	vs. Houston (Miller)	1
65.	September 23	at San Diego (Middlebrook)	0
66.	September 23	at San Diego (Middlebrook)	0
67.	September 24	at Los Angeles (Baldwin)	0
68.	September 28	vs. San Diego (Middlebrook)	0
69.	September 29	vs. San Diego (McElroy)	0
70.	October 4	at Houston (W.Rodriguez)	0
71.	October 5	vs. Los Angeles (Park)	0
72.	October 5	vs. Los Angeles (Park)	0
73.	October 7	vs. Los Angeles (Springer)	0

BROKEN RECORDS

A list of significant records and milestones broken or tied during the 2001 Major League Baseball season.

PLAYERS

BARRY BONDS • SAN FRANCISCO GIANTS

Broke Mark McGwire's record for most homeruns in one season (73).
Broke Babe Ruth's record for highest slugging percentage in a season (.863).
Broke Roger Maris' record for most homeruns in one season by a left-handed hitter.
Oldest player to lead the major leagues in homeruns (38).
Oldest player to hit 50, 60 and 70 home runs.
Broke the major-league record for walks in one season (177).
Only player to have two six-game homerun streaks in career.
Fastest player to 30, 40, 50, 60 and 70 homers in a season.
Most MVP awards (4)

ICHIRO SUZUKI • SEATTLE MARINERS

Third player since 1931 with at least 240 hits in a season (242).
Broke "Shoeless" Joe Jackson's Major League rookie record for hits in a season.
Broke Wade Boggs's American League record for most singles in a season (192).

ALBERT PUJOL • ST. LOUIS CARDINALS

Broke Wally Berger's National League rookie record for most RBIs (130).
Broke Johnny Frederick's National League rookie record for most extra-base hits (88).
Broke Richie Allen's National League rookie record for most total bases.

SAMMY SOSA • CHICAGO CUBS

His 17 homeruns tied Willie Mays' National League record for August.
First player to hit 60 homeruns in three different seasons.

RICKEY HENDERSON • SAN DIEGO PADRES

Broke Ty Cobb's Major League record of runs scored (2,248).
Broke Babe Ruth's Major League record for walks in a career (2,141).

RANDY JOHNSON • ARIZONA DIAMONDBACKS

Sixteen strikeouts in seven relief innings pitched set the record for a relief pitcher in a game.
First player to strikeout 300 batters in four straight seasons.

ROGER CLEMENS • NEW YORK YANKEES

First pitcher since 1900 to start season 20-1.
Broke Walter Johnson's American League record for most strikeouts in career (3,717).
First pitcher with two separate 16-game win streaks in a career.
Most Cy Young awards (6).

ALEX RODRIGUEZ • TEXAS RANGERS

Most homeruns in a season by a shortstop (52).

LANCE BERKMAN • HOUSTON ASTROS

First switch-hitter in history with 30 homeruns and 50 doubles in same season.
Most doubles in season by a switch hitter.

CAL RIPKEN JR. • BALTIMORE ORIOLES

Oldest player to hit a homerun in All-Star Game history (40).

TODD HELTON • COLORADO ROCKIES

First player with 100 extra-base hits in consecutive seasons.

JEFF BAGWELL • HOUSTON ASTROS

First player in history with at least 30 homeruns, 100 RBIs, 100 runs and 100 walks in six consecutive seasons.

TREVOR HOFFMAN • SAN DIEGO PADRES

First reliever with four straight 40-save seasons.
First reliever with five career 40-save seasons.

KAZ SASAKI • SEATTLE MARINERS

Broke Lee Smith's Major League record with 13 saves in April.

KEN GRIFFEY JR. • CINCINNATTI REDS

Youngest player to hit 450 career homeruns (31).

PAUL O'NEILL • NEW YORK YANKEES

Oldest player in history to have 20 homeruns and 20 stolen bases in same season (38).

JAMIE MOYER • SEATTLE MARINERS

Become oldest pitcher to win 20 games in a season for the first time (38).

LUIS GONZALEZ • SEATTLE MARINERS

Fastest player in Major League history to 20 homeruns in a season (40 games).

BRET BOONE • SEATTLE MARINERS

Broke Joe Gordon's American League record for homeruns in a season by a second baseman (37).
Broke Charlie Gehringer's American League record for RBIs in a season by a second baseman (141).

GREG MADDUX • ATLANTA BRAVES

Pitched 70 1/3 innings to break Christy Mathewson's and Randy Jones's National League record for most consecutive innings pitched without allowing a walk.

TEAMS

SEATTLE MARINERS

Broke 1906-07 Cubs record for longest unbeaten streak in consecutive road series (24).

Broke 1998 Yankees record for most wins in American League history (116).

Tied 1906 Cubs for most wins in a season (116).

OAKLAND A'S

Most wins in a season by a wild-card team (100).

ARIZONA DIAMONDBACKS

Quickest expansion team to win the World Series in modern era (four years).